What is prayer?

Why should I pray?

HOW and WHEN do I pray?

P9-EEF-854

What things should I pray about?

Why do people fold their hands and close their eyes when they pray?

Does a prayer have different parts to it?

Is a silent prayer as effective as a spoken one?

What is God like?

Is it important to pray with others?

Does God really care about our prayers?

Does God answer every prayer?

What can I do to make prayer more fun?

Millie's Prayer Projects

Fun & Creative
Ways to Pray

MCP
Mission City Press

Franklin, Tennessee

Millie's Prayer Projects: Fun and Creative Ways to Pray
Copyright © 2003, Mission City Press, Inc. All rights reserved.

Published by Mission City Press, Inc.

No part of this publication may be reproduced, stored in a retrieval system, or trans-mitted in any form or by any means—electronic, mechanical, photocopying, record-ing, or any other—without the prior written permission of the publisher.

Writers: Karen Wingate, Wendy Witherow, Beverly Elliott,
                and members of the girls club at www.alifeoffaith.com

Cover Design: Richmond & Williams, Nashville, TN
Cover Photography: Michelle Grisco Photography, West Covina, CA
Interior Design: NBishop, Tulsa, OK

Unless otherwise indicated, all Scripture references are from the *Holy Bible, New International Version* (NIV). Copyright © 1973, 1978, 1984, by International Bible Society. Used by permission of Zondervan Publishing House, Grand Rapids, MI. All rights reserved. Note: Where there are italics within a verse of Scripture, it is emphasis added by the writers of this book.

Millie Keith and *A Life of Faith* are trademarks of Mission City Press, Inc.

For more information, write to Mission City Press at P.O. Box 681913, Franklin, Tennessee 37068-1913, or visit our Web site at:

www.alifeoffaith.com

Library of Congress Catalog Card Number: 2002112022
Mission City Press
Millie's Prayer Projects: Fun and Creative Ways to Pray
ISBN 1-928749-58-5

Printed in the United States of America
1 2 3 4 5 6 7 8 — 07 06 05 04 03

This book is dedicated to:

Melissa Savage,
Kimmie Toth

and

Abigail Nesbitt

"You are the light of the world.
A city on a hill cannot be hidden."

Matthew 5:14

Table of Contents

Appendixes — Deeper Study

Introduction

Do you want to grow closer to God? Do you want your life of faith to be more exciting? Do you want wisdom from Heaven that will help you with the day-to-day issues of life? Do you want to feel continuously connected to God? Prayer is the key.

Millie's Prayer Projects will show you that prayer can be fun, creative, satisfying, and exciting! Through imaginative "prayer project" ideas submitted by members of the girls club at *www.alifeoffaith.com*, you will learn how to draw near to God with confidence. And as you encounter God through your prayers (and see Him working in marvelous ways through the answers to those prayers!), God will become more and more real to you. Soon you will find yourself living a vibrant, dynamic life of faith!

Developing a prayer life is one of the main ways you unlock the door to the great mysteries of God.

How to Use This Book

This book isn't just a book to read and then put away. This is an *activity* book. The brief, helpful teachings will help you understand various aspects of prayer and inspire you to come up with your own creative prayer ideas.

To help you, this book has the following features:

Prayer Ideas

Creative ideas for praying by yourself, with a friend, or with a group of friends.

Prayer Projects

Activities you can do by yourself, with a friend or group of friends, or with your family to make prayer more fun and exciting. Some of the activities are short; others are long and take more planning. You can mix them up or do them in order.

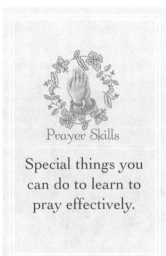

Prayer Skills

Special things you can do to learn to pray effectively.

Pictures of Prayer

Stories from the Bible that give you an illustration about prayer. Prayer is as relevant to you today as it was to the characters of Bible days!

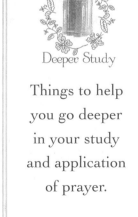

Deeper Study

Things to help you go deeper in your study and application of prayer.

A Helpful Hint

As you spend time in *Millie's Prayer Projects*, you will find it beneficial to have a prayer notebook or journal in which to record your prayers and answers to prayer. Several ideas for how to make your own prayer journal are included in this book, or you can purchase a copy of *Millie's Daily Diary*—a journal designed especially for girls who want to live a life of faith. It has the unique feature of tabbed sections so that entries can be made in different categories. Besides plenty of space to write daily reflections, there are separate sections for recording your prayers, answers to prayer, favorite Scriptures, and more. And it is full of beautiful color photos of Millie!

A Life of Adventure

"God calls us to a wild adventure, not a tea party, my dear," said Aunt Wealthy to Millie Keith. *Millie's Courageous Days*, page 17

If you have read the Millie Keith novels—the stories of a young girl growing up on the American frontier in the 1830s—then you know that a life of faith is a life of adventure—a grand adventure. It is wilder and more awesome than any roller coaster you've ever ridden.

Millie-Style Scrapbook
by Rachel C. and Beverly E.

Prayer Projects

Make a prayer scrapbook like Millie might have made. You will need a blank photo album or scrapbook, paper (plain or colored), magazine pictures, and a picture from the Millie web site for the cover. Fill your scrapbook with mementos of your life. You can: write a journal entry like the entries Millie might have written, pouring your heart out to God; write a letter to a relative—as Millie would've written to Aunt Wealthy—about an issue for which you need wise counsel; draw a picture from one of your prayer walks (Millie liked to draw the animals she saw!); draw your family tree and use it as a "prayer tree" to remind you to pray for your family and relatives (see the family tree in the Millie books); draw pictures that represent your friends and list some things to pray for each one (Millie loved to pray for her friends!); make a list of people who need to know God's love—especially people you find hard to love, like Damaris Drybread was for Millie—and pray regularly for them; and add pictures throughout your scrapbook that represent the historical time period in which you live.

Picture Prayer Journal
by Cora L., age 10

This is a fun and easy way to pray! And it also helps you know whom to pray for or what to pray for! It's easy! The supplies you need are: a photo album or three-ring binder, page protectors, art supplies to decorate the album, and notebook paper. Ask your parents to let you use pictures of different family members (either real pictures, photocopies, or pictures scanned into a computer then printed with a color inkjet printer).

Place one picture per page in the photo album or in a page protector. On your notebook paper, write down prayers for each person, and then insert the paper underneath the picture of that person. You could also use pictures of our nation's leaders clipped from newspapers or magazines and include them in your prayer album. Ask God whom He wants you to pray for.

You can also use a shoebox for this prayer project. Using your pictures, write your prayer for each person on a sticky note and put it on the back of each person's picture. Then put the pictures in the box. When you are ready to pray, pick two pictures out of the shoebox and pray for those two people.

When God answers a particular prayer request, write on the sticky note how He did it! Don't forget to put the date when you start to pray and when your prayer request is answered. See how long it takes! And before you know it, you might have to take more pictures! I pray that this will help you, and I pray that God will answer your prayers soon! But if He doesn't, don't give up; He will, one way or another!

The scenery from the top is spectacular. Sometimes the ride seems faster than you can stand. You never know what might be around the next corner, but the ride sure is thrilling!

A roller-coaster ride, however, is not a one-person adventure, is it? There's always a seat for two, and it's certainly more fun when you share the experience with a friend. You hold hands, scream at the scary parts, grasp one another tightly, and excitedly agree to try it again.

Can you imagine getting on the ride with your friend and not laughing and screaming together through the twists and turns, the climbing of the car and the plunging back down again? Can you imagine not talking to your friend about the exciting experience once the ride is over? Of course not!

Well, the roller coaster of your life is not meant to be ridden alone. You are meant to ride hand in hand with God, your Creator. He wants to go on your journey of faith with you! He wants to be there every step of the way. And as you travel on this wild adventure, He longs to talk with you, to listen to you, and to hold you tightly to His side when the ride gets bumpy or scary. He wants to point out all of the wonderful sights along the way. He wants to make special memories with you!

Talking with God throughout the ride is what we call prayer. Prayer isn't boring at all. Like your walk of faith, prayer is an exciting journey with twists and turns, spectacular views, and wonderful surprises. Prayer is a multifaceted, uplifting, awe-inspiring adventure!

Are you ready for a fantastic ride? Take time now to say "hello" to the One who created you. He is anxious for you to know Him better, and He has many things to share with you as you explore a life of prayer together.

What Is Prayer?

The definition of prayer is simple. Prayer is talking to God. Prayer is talking to God just as easily as you would talk to your parents or a close friend.

But wait a minute! Think about the Person on the other end of your conversation. God is the One who made the entire universe and everything in it, including you! He is the source of all wisdom, perfection, and goodness. He

Prayer Journal
by Amanda C., age 16

Prayer Projects

My friend and I each made our own prayer journals together. We made the covers out of colored paper folded in half. Next we folded computer paper in half, inserting the pages inside the cover, so the folds fit together. Then we stapled the book together along the fold. We each decorated our cover and wrote a Bible verse on the front. You can make it that way or just be creative—make it your own way!

My friend wrote her prayer requests in the front of my prayer journal, and I wrote my requests in the middle. We did the same with hers—mine in the front and hers in the middle. Then we would get together at least once a week and go through the book and tell each other about the answers to our prayers. It was really neat to see how much God did through us by our simply praying together!

knows every single thing about you—including how many hairs are on your head. He loves you, and He wants you to talk to Him. He wants to talk with you too. He delights to hear about your good days and bad days, your ups and downs. Like a loving father, He wants you to tell Him what you need, what you are excited about, and what is troubling you. He longs to share the secrets of His love and His truth with you.

> This is what the LORD says, he who made the earth, the LORD who formed it and established it—the LORD is his name: "Call to me and I will answer you and tell you great and unsearchable things you do not know." —JEREMIAH 33:2–3

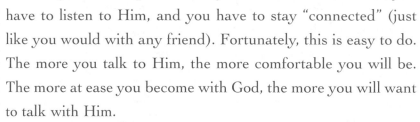

Why Pray?

The reason we pray is to strengthen and develop our relationship with God. It is very simple. If you want a strong relationship with God, you have to talk with Him, you have to listen to Him, and you have to stay "connected" (just like you would with any friend). Fortunately, this is easy to do. The more you talk to Him, the more comfortable you will be. The more at ease you become with God, the more you will want to talk with Him.

Prayer is like glue that holds your relationship with God together!

Think about how you talk with your best friends. The more comfortable you are with your friends, the more time you want to spend talking to them—either in person, on the phone, or through e-mail. As you get to know God better, you will want to spend more time talking with Him too.

When you have a close prayer relationship with God, you'll discover that He is with you all the time, ready to help you and protect you, ready to give you strength and wisdom, ready to help you live a life of faith. All you have to do is ask!

Before You Pray

Since prayer is talking with God, the first step is to have a relationship with Him. The Bible says that you—and all human beings—have sinned and fallen short of God's standards of holiness (see Romans 3:23). This has broken the relationship between you and Him. The only way for your relationship with God to be restored is through Jesus Christ. It was His death and resurrection that paid the penalty for your sins and the sins of mankind.

If you have not accepted the gift of salvation that Jesus offers you, we encourage you to make this your first step as you seek God through prayer. To help you, we have said more about this important first step at the end of this book in Appendix G. There is even a simple prayer that you can pray. God's wonderful gift of salvation is **free.**

All you have to do is accept it! Don't wait another minute!

If you confess with your mouth, "Jesus is Lord," and believe in your heart that God raised him from the dead, you will be saved.

—ROMANS 10:9

Prayer Projects

Simple Prayer Journal
by Kara H., age 10

Some of you may have used a prayer journal before. If you haven't, you can easily make your own. What you need is a binder, lined papers, tape, a piece of drawing paper, and a picture. First, put the lined papers in the binder. Then tape the drawing paper on the front of the binder. Last, tape the picture onto the drawing paper.

Requests-and-Answers Journal
by Elizabeth S. and Susan S.

Draw a line down the middle of each page of a journal. Label the left column "Requests" and the right column "Answers." Keep a record of your requests, remembering to be specific in your requests to God. When God answers a particular prayer, write the answer in the right column. Praise God for His answers.

Millie's Prayer Life

Millie Keith was a young woman who knew the value and importance of prayer. For Millie, talking to God was as easy as confiding in a best friend. And that's exactly who God was to Millie—her very best friend!

You can learn a lot by looking at Millie's faithful prayer life. And as you do, you will see that talking to God isn't as hard or as mysterious as you might think. A prayer life with God is natural, comforting, and very exciting.

> The LORD confides in those who fear him; he makes his covenant known to them.
>
> —Psalm 25:14

First, let's talk about where Millie prayed. You might be surprised. Millie talked to God in all kinds of places. For instance, Millie talked to God in a secluded garden, hiding herself among the lilac blooms. In a crowded room of people, Millie would lift up silent prayers to her Lord, just as if He were by her side, which in fact He was. When Millie's family traveled by boat to their new home in Pleasant Plains, Millie talked to God in their dark sleeping quarters. She also talked to Him on the sunny deck of the boat. She prayed in her bedroom—morning and night. Millie also prayed while she was taking a walk, cooking, sewing, and drawing in her sketchbook. We even see her talking to God when she was right in the middle of a conflict with her mischievous brothers. Millie prayed anywhere—anytime! Talking to God was a normal part of Millie's everyday life.

But what did Millie pray to God about? Millie prayed about many of the same issues that today's young girls deal with. She prayed about her daily circumstances, her living conditions, and her wants and needs. She prayed about the pressures she faced—like trying to fit in with the other kids and standing up against gossip. She prayed about people in her life who were hard for her to like, let alone love. Millie prayed when she found out that she was moving to the frontier, when her family became sick, when her best friend rejected her because of her faith, when she was nervous about meeting new people, and when she was furious with her mischievous little brothers.

In other words, Millie talked to God about everything—whatever was on her mind or in her heart. She told God about all of her frustrations, fears, likes, dislikes, struggles, weaknesses, goals, and dreams, whether big or small. She talked to Him when she was happy and when she was sad. Millie prayed short prayers, and she prayed long prayers.

Millie was very open with God, and the more honest she was with Him, the more He changed her heart and helped her become loving, patient, and wise. She let God know when she didn't understand His Word or what He was doing in her life. And she often prayed Scripture verses back to God—reminding herself and reminding Him of His promises. Millie prayed and sought God's solutions to every problem in life, and He always proved Himself faithful to her—sometimes in the most unexpected ways.

But Millie didn't talk with God just to share her burdens and needs. Millie also asked God questions. She was eager to know what He was thinking and feeling. She often talked with Him simply to let Him know how much she loved Him and that she was thinking of Him. Millie had a true friendship with God.

When did Millie talk to God? Millie talked to Him throughout her day. She talked to Him first thing in the morning. Then at nighttime, alone in her room, Millie often had long conversations with God, searching her Bible and writing in her journal.

Why was it so easy for Millie to pray? Because she knew how much God loved her. She knew that prayer was vital to her growing relationship with Him. Millie knew that He had the wisdom to help her, and she also knew how important it was to simply enjoy His companionship. Millie found great comfort and strength in her conversations with God. Prayer was a part of Millie's *lifestyle*. Prayer was Millie's *lifeline*.

Chapter 1
Talking with God

Have you ever walked into a room where you were a stranger and had to intro-duce yourself to someone you didn't know? It can be a little unnerving. Or have you ever seen someone at school or church who was clearly a newcomer? You may have found it difficult to approach them. That's because whether you are the newcomer or not, getting to know someone new feels a little awkward at first. But once you get past those awkward first words, you can begin to reap the rewards of friendship.

Approaching God with Confidence

Perhaps you have felt a little nervous praying. Or you felt timid or shy with God, and it was hard to get started. If you don't know God well, talking to Him may seem uncomfortable at first. But the death and resurrection of Jesus on your behalf gives you the privilege of approaching God the Father with confidence. There is no need to be nervous or unsure.

Hebrews 10:19, 22 says, "Since we have *confidence* to enter the Most Holy Place by the blood of Jesus … let us draw near to God with a sincere heart *in full assurance of faith.*" That means that you can come to God with the *assurance* that He will warmly receive you and be interested in hearing everything you have to say!

Roles and Relationships

Prayer Skills

Would you talk to your best friend the way you would to your little brother? Probably not. Behavior, tone of voice, and attitude often change from person to person. You probably have many relationships with different types of people. How you relate to them differs depending on their role in your life, how highly you regard them in that role, and how close you are to them.

This activity will cause you to think about how you talk and communicate with other people and, ultimately, make you more aware of how you communicate with God. Go through the following list and imagine having a conversation with each of the people mentioned, or grab a friend and role play. Pay attention to the words you choose, your tone of voice, and even the body language you use with each person. Note how your respect and intimacy vary from person to person, depending upon the role and your relationship with the person you're speaking to.

You and the school principal

You and the queen of England

You and a great-aunt you've just met for the first time

You and the president of the United States

You and God

You and your best friend

You and your little sister

You and your older sister

You and your mom

You and your grandmother

Hebrews 4:14–16 says:

> Since we have a great high priest who has gone through the heavens, Jesus the Son of God, let us hold firmly to the faith we profess. For we do not have a high priest who is unable to sympathize with our weaknesses, but we have one who has been tempted in every way, just as we are—yet was without sin. Let us then approach the throne of grace with confidence, so that we may receive mercy and find grace to help us in our time of need.

You can approach the throne of grace *with confidence*! That means you don't need to feel shy. When you pray, you can leave timidity and insecurity behind, for God understands even your weaknesses! He wants to give you grace and mercy. He *wants* you to come to Him with your needs.

In the Name of Jesus

We've talked about how Jesus makes it possible for us to have access to God. You might say that Jesus' name is like a ticket that allows you to go into God the Father's presence anytime you choose. Without that ticket (Jesus), you wouldn't even get through the door.

> Jesus answered, "I am the way and the truth and the life. No one comes to the Father except through me."   —JOHN 14:6

The Bible teaches that when we pray, we are to pray to God the Father "in the name of Jesus." That's because the name of Jesus is the most powerful name in the universe, and when you use the name of Jesus in your prayers, it brings glory to God.

> Being found in appearance as a man, he (Jesus) humbled himself and became obedient to death—even death on a cross! Therefore God exalted him to the highest place and gave him the name that is above every name, that at the name of Jesus every knee should bow, in heaven and on earth and under the earth, and every tongue confess that Jesus Christ is Lord, to the glory of God the Father. —PHILIPPIANS 2:8–11

The Help of the Holy Spirit

As a human being, you have a body and a soul, but you also have a spirit. God is a spirit, and since He is holy, His Spirit is called the "Holy Spirit." What does the Holy Spirit have to do with prayer?

Before Jesus went to the Cross, He promised His disciples that after His death and resurrection, God the Father would send them a Helper: "I will ask the Father, and he will give you another Counselor to be with you forever—the Spirit of truth. The world cannot accept him, because it neither sees him nor knows him. But you know him, for he lives with you and will be in you" (John 14:16–17). Jesus went on to say, "The Counselor, the Holy Spirit, whom the Father will send in my name, will teach you all things and will remind you of everything I have said to you"—JOHN 14:26.

ROMANS 8:26–27 says: In the same way, the Spirit helps us in our weakness. We do not know what we ought to pray for, but the Spirit himself intercedes for us with groans that words cannot express. And he who searches our hearts knows the mind of the Spirit, because the Spirit intercedes for the saints in accordance with God's will.

Our Awesome God!

Have you ever wondered what God is like or what is going on up in Heaven where He dwells? In the book of Revelation, John the apostle had an amazing experience: he was able to glimpse into Heaven and see what human eyes do not get the opportunity to see. Here is what John said:

Pictures of Prayer

REVELATION 4:1–11

I looked, and there before me was a door standing open in heaven. And the voice I had first heard speaking to me like a trumpet said, "Come up here, and I will show you what must take place after this."

At once I was in the Spirit, and there before me was a throne in heaven with someone sitting on it. And the one who sat there had the appearance of jasper and carnelian. A rainbow, resembling an emerald, encircled the throne. Surrounding the throne were twenty-four other thrones, and seated on them were twenty-four elders. They were dressed in white and had crowns of gold on their heads.

From the throne came flashes of lightning, rumblings and peals of thunder. Before the throne, seven lamps were blazing. These are the seven spirits of God. Also before the

If you are a Christian, the Holy Spirit of God lives within you and He is there to pray for you (to "intercede" for you) and to help you pray—especially when you don't know what you ought to pray for. Do not be afraid to ask for help!

throne there was what looked like a sea of glass, clear as crystal. In the center, around the throne, were four living creatures, and they were covered with eyes, in front and in back. The first living creature was like a lion, the second was like an ox, the third had a face like a man, the fourth was like a flying eagle. Each of the four living creatures had six wings and was covered with eyes all around, even under his wings. Day and night they never stop saying: "Holy, holy, holy is the Lord God Almighty, who was, and is, and is to come."

Whenever the living creatures give glory, honor and thanks to him who sits on the throne and who lives for ever and ever, the twenty-four elders fall down before him who sits on the throne, and worship him who lives for ever and ever. They lay their crowns before the throne and say: "You are worthy, our Lord and God, to receive glory and honor and power, for you created all things, and by your will they were created and have their being."

As you can see from John's description, God is very powerful and important. In His presence there is intense praise and worship, adoration, fear, and awe. He is so mighty—He is holy, and He loves you very deeply and tenderly. He wants to know you personally.

What Is God Like?

Let's dig a little deeper into the subject of *Who* is listening to us when we pray. What is He like? What can we know about Him that will help us with our prayers?

God Is Almighty

God's nature has many aspects. He can be the frightful Lion of Judah or the meek Lamb of God. He is the tender, compassionate Papa, and He is the Ruler of the Universe! He is the King of Kings and the Lord of Lords. There is no power greater than His. When the apostle John saw the vision of the glorified Christ mentioned in Revelation 1, he fell to the floor like a dead man. God's magnificence and holiness is overwhelming!

It is easy to treat God like a school buddy or a talking partner, but He is so much more. He is the All-Powerful, Almighty, Holy God—the Ruler of All, the King of Kings and the Lord of Lords. God is *far* more powerful than the queen of England or the president of the United States or any other world leader. That's why when you come to God, it's important to come before Him with humility, reverence, and adoration.

Praying to God is like entering the grandest throne room imaginable, with God Almighty seated on the most glorious throne. However, if we have Jesus in our hearts, we don't have to be nervous about coming before Him.

Though we are full of honor and respect for the awesomeness of God, we must know that we can approach His throne *with confidence and boldness* because of Jesus, who has gone ahead of us and made a way for us.

The Throne Room of God

Prayer Ideas

Have you ever taken a tour of a palace, a mansion, a beautiful museum, or perhaps a fancy hotel with marble floors, high ceilings, big pillars, statues, oil paintings, and gold decorations? The beauty of those places does not even begin to compare with the majesty of God and Heaven. The Bible refers to the "glorious splendor" of God's majesty.

As you get ready to pray, take some time to imagine yourself standing in the throne room of God. Perhaps the sides of the room are flanked with mighty warriors and resplendent courtiers. On the throne sits God, the most awesome, glorious, regal Person you have ever seen. Light, music, power, and authority flow from the mighty throne. It is absolute magnificence! You feel so small, so insignificant, so . . . almost afraid. As you force your eyes to look at the floor, the King holds out His hand. "Come, my daughter," He bids. You walk to Him—slowly at first and then hurrying. He takes your hand and you stand close to Him beside His great throne, pouring your heart out to Him, aware that even as you speak, He already knows all about your situation and He is guiding you and comforting you with His continual presence.

Draw a picture in your prayer journal of what you imagine the throne room of God to be like, or write down your own description of it. Then in your own words, express to God your awe at what you see and feel.

The LORD made the heavens. Splendor and majesty are before him; strength and joy in his dwelling place. Ascribe to the LORD, O families of nations, ascribe to the LORD glory and strength, ascribe to the LORD the glory due his name. Bring an offering and come before him; worship the LORD in the splendor of his holiness.

1 Chronicles 16:26–29

God Is a Person

When you pray, you aren't speaking into the air. You aren't just talking or thinking to yourself. You aren't just connecting sentences that sound good together. You are talking to a real live Person who is listening intently to every word you say. This Person is God, your Creator. He can be anywhere and everywhere—at the same time. He knows everything about everyone, and He knows all that is happening in the world at each moment. God is awesome! He deserves your sincerity and your full attention.

God is a Spirit, but He is also a Person who wants you to relate to Him. To help you, He uses language that you can understand. That is why the Bible is full of passages

Gifts for the King

Prayer Ideas

In Matthew 2:1–11, we read the story of the birth of Jesus and the Magi from the east who came to worship "the one who has been born king of the Jews." When they found the child with His mother, they bowed down and worshiped Him and gave Him gifts of gold, incense, and myrrh. Because He was a king, they wanted to honor Him by bringing Him things that were of value to them.

Think about what things are of value to you that you could present to King Jesus as gifts. Then kneel down in a quiet place. Close your eyes and be still, quieting your mind. Then imagine yourself bowing down before Jesus, the King of Kings. Tell Him in prayer how much you love Him and reverently offer Him one of your gifts. It might be a favorite book, a doll or stuffed animal, or even a relationship that you cherish. Or it might be the gift of your heart. Share with Him why that gift is special to you and what it means to you to give it to Him. Then speak to Him words of honor and adoration, such as the following:

1 Chronicles 29:11–13

Yours, O LORD, is the greatness and the power and the glory and the majesty and the splendor, for everything in heaven and earth is yours. Yours, O LORD, is the kingdom; you are exalted as head over all. Wealth and honor come from you; you are the ruler of all things. In your hands are strength and power to exalt and give strength to all. Now, our God, [I] give you thanks, and praise your glorious name.

referring to Him with ears, eyes, hands, arms, feet, face, a back, nostrils, mouth, etc. Here are some places where God described *Himself* in terms of physical characteristics:

My own hand laid the foundations of the earth, and my right hand spread out the heavens. —ISAIAH 48:13

The glory of Lebanon will come to you, the pine, the fir and the cypress together, to adorn the place of my sanctuary; and I will glorify the place of my feet. —ISAIAH 60:13

Then the LORD said, "There is a place near me where you may stand on a rock. When my glory passes by, I will put you in a cleft in the rock and cover you with my hand until I have passed by. Then I will remove my hand and you will see my back; but my face must not be seen." —EXODUS 33:21–23

God knows that as humans, we have a very limited ability to comprehend Him, so He refers to human characteristics in order to give us a picture we can understand—so that we can relate to Him better and visualize Him in a way that is familiar to us. Try using some of these descriptions about God when you pray.

For example, if you need help, ask God to stretch out His mighty arm to rescue you. If you want to ask Him something important, ask Him to open His ears to hear your request. If you need Him to give attention to a certain matter, ask Him to turn His eyes upon you—to fix His gaze upon your situation.

Remember, the more you get to know God, the more you will love to talk with Him.

Divine Imaginations

Prayer Ideas

God has given you a wonderful gift of imagination. Don't be afraid to use it when you pray! Let the graphic description of the glorified Christ given in Revelation 1:12–16 inspire your imagination as you pray and worship. You will see that John described God's feet, chest, head and hair, eyes, voice, right hand, mouth, and face:

I turned around to see the voice that was speaking to me. And when I turned I saw seven golden lampstands, and among the lampstands was someone "like a son of man," dressed in a robe reaching down to his *feet* and with a golden sash around his *chest*. His *head and hair* were white like wool, as white as snow, and his *eyes* were like blazing fire. His *feet* were like bronze glowing in a furnace, and his *voice* was like the sound of rushing waters. In his *right hand* he held seven stars, and out of his *mouth* came a sharp double-edged sword. His *face* was like the sun shining in all its brilliance.
(Revelation 1:12–16)

God Has a Personality

God has given us many detailed descriptions of His "personality." His nature and His character are described throughout His Word. For example, in Exodus, we read this:

Exodus 34:5–7 — The LORD came down in the cloud and stood there with (Moses) and proclaimed his name, the LORD. And he passed in front of Moses, proclaiming, "The LORD, the LORD, the compassionate and gracious God, slow to anger, abounding in love and faithfulness, maintaining love to thousands, and forgiving wickedness, rebellion and sin."

The Bible also gives us these other images:

The name of the LORD is a strong tower; the righteous run to it and are safe. — PROVERBS 18:10

The LORD is my shepherd, I shall not be in want. He makes me lie down in green pastures, he leads me beside quiet waters, he restores my soul. He guides me in paths of righteousness for his name's sake. — PSALM 23:1–3

One of the elders said to me, "Do not weep! See, the Lion of the tribe of Judah, the Root of David, has triumphed". — REVELATION 5:5

If you feel frightened, picture God as a strong fortress. Run and hide inside! If you need comfort, picture Him as a compassionate

Shepherd holding you tenderly as one of His precious little lambs. If you need protection from evil, think of Him as the terrible and mighty Lion of Judah roaring at your adversary.

Just as you grow closer to a friend the more you spend time with her, prayer will help you grow closer and closer to God!

God Is a Father

We have learned so far that God is Almighty and very powerful. Heaven is filled with worship and adoration to Him because of His greatness and complete holiness. We have also seen that God is a Person with an incredible personality.

But the most tender impression of all is of God as Father. God wants you to know Him as a Father—your Heavenly Father. Romans 8:15 says you are a child of God and can address Him as "Abba, Father," which is translated as "Daddy" or "Papa." This is so very personal and intimate. He wants to relate to you in an affectionate and loving manner.

Picture God as your Daddy and yourself as His child. He wants you to run to Him just as a child would to his or her loving earthly daddy. Read Psalm 139 out loud. Psalm 139 shows how much your Daddy knows and cares about you. He knows everything you are thinking and how you are feeling. Verse 3 says that He is very familiar with all of your ways,

Praising God from A to Z

Prayer Ideas

Just as you want people to know you for who you really are on the inside, God wants people to know Him for who He really is too. He has feelings and desires and emotions and opinions. He has many wonderful characteristics. You can never know everything about God—no one can—but there are many things you can tell about Him from His Word.

Search your Bible and see how many different words you can come up with to describe God. For each letter of the alphabet, list adjectives, words, or phrases that describe God's nature or character. Work on the list with your friends after school, with your family at home, or while you travel in the car (for help, see the list in Appendix D titled, "The Nature and Character of God From A to Z").

Then praise God using the alphabet. Start by thanking Him for who and what He is that begins with the letter **A** (such as "abounding in love"). Then praise Him for being something that begins with the letter **B** (such as "brilliant"), then **C** (such as "compassionate"). Continue until you have gone through the entire alphabet!

Isaiah Project

Prayer Ideas

Read Isaiah, chapters 40–66. Record in your prayer notebook what you learn about the character of God. Each time you write something down, thank God that He possesses that characteristic. For example, Isaiah 41:10 promises that God will be with you, strengthen you, and help you. Pray something like: "Lord, thank You for always being with me. I praise You because You have the power to help me when I need it."

Secret Love Notes

Prayer Projects

God your Abba Father loves you so much! You are always on His heart and mind. If you could hear in the spirit all the time, you would hear Him saying, "I love you, my child," constantly. Unfortunately all the noise and distractions in life tend to drown out God's love messages. So try this prayer project: whenever you see a beautiful sunset, a flag flying, or something else of your choosing, or perhaps whenever you hear a particular sound, such as a bird singing, consider it a love note to you from your Heavenly Father. No matter where you are or what you are doing at the time, stop and take a minute to ponder God's great love for you. Then say, "I love You too." You will be surprised at how many love notes God sends you!

and verse 17 says that He thinks about you so much that you couldn't begin to add up all His thoughts of you. Verses 7–10 beautifully declare that His presence is always with you. After reading Psalm 139, you will become acutely aware that your Father God lovingly created you, knows you perfectly well, will never leave you, and will care for you always. That should make you want to run to Him and tell Him everything!

God is a better father than the very best of all earthly fathers, and like any good father, God loves to give His children good gifts. Matthew 7:11 says, "If you, then, though you are evil, know how to give good gifts to your children, how much more will your Father in heaven give good gifts to those who ask him!"

God has given you everything—life, breath, and blessings in abundance. He has made the whole universe. It belongs to Him. It is His to share with you, and He does so gladly because He loves you so much. "Every good and perfect gift is from above, coming down from the Father of the heavenly lights, who does not change like shifting shadows," says James 1:17. God delights in giving you good things.

God's Occupations

Prayer Ideas

To enjoy praying to God, you need to get to know all about Him. You know that God is the Creator of the heavens and the earth, darkness and light, silence and sound, the plants, the animals, the sky, the land, the sea, and all of mankind. He designed all of their characteristics down to the smallest detail. Have you ever thought about how that makes God a designer, an artist, a sculptor, a painter, a decorator, a gardener, a landscaper, an architect, a builder, a manufacturer, a composer, a hair-dresser, a biologist, and a zoologist?

On top of that, God made the sun, the moon, the stars, the planets, the galaxies, etc. He assigned each of them their own positions and made them all exist together in perfect harmony—which was no small feat! He created time, established day and night, developed seasons, and made them work together like clockwork! (Even the seasons know just when they are supposed to change!) And God did the same thing for your human body: He created each and every part—including organs, cells, and ligaments—and made them all work together in unity and in constant communication with one another. That says that God is a programmer, a systems analyst, an astronomer, a scientist, a mathematician, a physicist, an engineer, a doctor, a dentist, and an inventor!

As the source of all wisdom, God is a teacher, a tutor, a trainer, and a counselor. As the One who oversees all of human history, God is also a producer and a director, a coach and a conductor. The Bible says that He is also a judge and a legislator, but since Jesus is your advocate, He is also a lawyer. He is your priest, your pastor, and your commander-in-chief. And He is your Heavenly Father, which makes Him a parent! And since all sixty-six books of the Bible were inspired by God, that means that God is also an author and a writer.

Those are just a few of God's occupations. There are many, many more. So the next time you are looking for a fun, new way to pray, talk to God about one of His professions!

The Names of God

Did you know that God has many special names and titles? We get to know our friends by taking an interest in who they are and what they are like. There might be some things you don't know about God. Show God you are really interested in getting to know Him by taking time to study the many names He possesses. This will give you great insight into your Best Friend! The following essay, as well as the additional names listed in Appendix E, will get you started!

The Names of God
by Katherine F., age 15

"What's in a name?" Everyone has a name, like Katie or Jessica or Elizabeth. What's the purpose of your name? To help people identify you. But what happens when, say, you and your cousin both have the same first name? Catholics often name all of their daughters Mary and then give them each a different middle name, like Mary Margaret and Mary Catherine. The purpose of this middle name is also to identify each person as clearly as possible. In the old days, people were given nicknames based on their occupation (John Baker), interesting abilities they had (what do you think of Tom Wiggle-Ears?), or where they lived (Mary Woods).

Abba Father What about God? Does God have any other names? Yes, He does! Even though we usually hear names like God, Jesus, and Lord more often than anything else, God has some specific names for special purposes. Just as your mother might call you by a nickname to express affection, Jesus called His Father "Abba, Father." This is an endearing term from a child to a father and shows how close Jesus felt to His Heavenly Parent.

Jesus has a name not quite as well known but still often heard: Emmanuel. *Emmanuel* means "God with us." Whenever people called Jesus by this name, they were to remember that God cared about them enough to send His Son to earth to be with them.

What's the first name of God that is ever used in the Bible? Nope…it's not *God*. Have you ever heard the name *Elohim*? It means "God as a Creator." The first verse of the first chapter of the first book of the Bible says this: "In the beginning God [Elohim] created the heavens and the earth." The word *El* means "mighty" and is used in reference to gods, especially our Almighty God. The ending of *Elohim* has a significant plural ending that means "there is more than one." But it does not mean that the *gods* created the heavens and the earth. *No*! It means that God the Father, God the Son, and God the Holy Spirit worked together as the Trinity to create this universe. Not only did Elohim create all of those different galaxies and planets, He also created the people on this earth. In Psalm 139:14 David, king of Israel, wrote, "I praise you because I am fearfully and wonderfully made; your works are wonderful, I know that full well."

Prayer Banners

Prayer Projects

Choose your favorite name or image of God, and write it on fabric, colored poster board, or canvas to make a banner you can hang in your room. Decorate it with beads, buttons, jewels, fancy trim, fabric paint, stitched-on pictures, and other items. For example, your banner might be made of purple fabric with gold lettering that reads "Jesus the Lamb of God" and a lamb sitting in a green pasture stitched underneath the wording. Or your banner might have angels and stars in the sky and the message "Christ Our Savior." Using fabric paint, you can even write out the passage found in Luke 2:14, which describes the angels announcing Jesus' birth.

El Roi. What does this mean? This name means "the God who sees." What does He see? He saw Hagar when she ran away from her mistress, Sarai (see Genesis 16:6–8). He sees you when you are hurting. Perhaps you feel that nobody understands you—or no one cares. You can run to El Roi and pray for help—He will help you!

Adonai means "Lord, Master, and Owner." But Adonai is a loving Master, one who will watch over you as you obey His commands.

Jehovah means "the self-existent One, the I AM." It is used more than 6,800 times in the Bible! Moses learned this name while flat on His face before God. The Jews considered it the most sacred of all of God's names—so sacred, in fact, that they wouldn't even say it. Some went so far as to take a complete ritual bath before writing the name Jehovah (if they ever had to), and they would write the name using a brand-new pen. Aren't you glad that we as Christians don't have to do all that? We can say this name out loud whenever we need help. God is so good! This name is so important that the names below are built upon this one.

Jehovah-Jireh means "the Lord will provide." Jehovah-Jireh prevented Isaac from being sacrificed on Mount Moriah and provided a ram to be sacrificed in his place. Jehovah-Jireh also sent His Son into the world to be our sacrifice. God has provided a substitute for us, so we will not need to die for our sins. But we need to reach out and accept His provision.

Jehovah-Rapha means "the Lord who heals." God heals all of us—our bodies, our emotions, and our souls. He brings healing when we are sick, salvation to our sin-ravaged souls, and soothing when we bring our hurts to Him. Jeremiah 17:14 says, "Heal me, O LORD, and I will be healed; save me and I will be saved, for you are the one I praise."

Jehovah-Nissi means "the Lord my banner." You may wonder, *Why in the world do I need a banner?* In the ancient times, warring armies brought a banner or pennant into battle. During the battle, they would look up to the flag, and if it was still held high, they would continue to fight with courage and confidence. The Lord will be your confidence when you encounter "battles" in your life as well! Jehovah-Nissi is your banner who will *always* be held high for you!

Jehovah-Shalom means "the Lord is peace." The name does not mean "the Lord is bringing peace," nor does it mean "the Lord was peace." It means "the Lord *is* peace"! He will bring you peace as you trust in Him.

Jehovah-Raah means "the Lord is my Shepherd." Most of us are very familiar with Psalm 23. But do you know what a shepherd does? Sheep are not known for their brains—as a matter of fact, sheep are pretty stupid. A flock of sheep without a shepherd would be completely helpless. But with Jehovah-Raah as our Shepherd, there is truly nothing we shall want! May the Lord bless you as you continue to seek Him!

Chapter 2
Making Time to Pray

Since God through His Holy Spirit lives inside you and is with you constantly, you can talk to God at any time and in any place. You don't have to make an appointment with Him. You don't have to wait in line until others are finished talking to Him. You don't have to wait until He's finished solving "bigger problems." He is *always* available to you.

You also don't have to wait until your regularly scheduled devotion time to bring your needs before God the Father. God doesn't say, "Wait! It's not 7:00 in the morning when you normally have your prayer time. Come back tomorrow." Because He is available anytime, you can always choose to take a few moments from your busy day to speak with your Heavenly Father and Friend.

How We Spend Our Time

Prayer Skills

Each day we have things we do at a certain time. We'll call that *scheduled time*. We also do things that have to be done within a certain time span, but we choose when we'll do them or how quickly we do them. This might include getting ready for school in the morning or doing homework in the evening. This is called *flexible time*. The rest of the time, which is *free time*, is ours to do whatever we want. The phrase *time management* means that each of us has to manage the limited time we have.

Let's see how you manage your time—how you spend the limited time you have each day. Get out your prayer notebook. Down the left side of a blank page, make a list of the hours from 6:00 A.M. to 10:00 P.M.—one hour on each line. Divide the page into seven columns and label each with the name of a different day of the week. Then fill out the chart as follows: with one color of pen or pencil, shade in the hours that are already scheduled (such as school, meals, and music lessons); with another color of pen or pencil, shade in the hours that are flexible. Leave blank the hours that are free time.

This activity will help you see how you spend your free time and what hours are already filled up in your day. Look for a good time in your day that you can spend talking with God. You might have to rearrange something else to carve out time for Him, but it will be well worth it.

The Bible says clearly that God is *always* with you. Look at the following promises:

Have I not commanded you? Be strong and courageous. Do not be terrified; do not be discouraged, for the LORD your God will be with you wherever you go. —JOSHUA 1:9

The LORD himself goes before you and will be with you; he will never leave you nor forsake you. Do not be afraid; do not be discouraged. —DEUTERONOMY 31:8

[Jesus said,] "Surely I am with you always, to the very end of the age." —MATTHEW 28:20

Since God is always with you, He is always able to hear you when you talk to Him and He is *always* listening. His schedule is never too busy for you. Can you fit Him into your busy schedule?

> As a teenage girl, I know that we face many pressures in life, both big and small. It helps when we pray for strength and courage to do the right thing. God never tires of helping us and hearing us out. In Ephesians 6:18, it says to "pray in the Spirit on all occasions." So A.S.A.P. (Always Say A Prayer) whenever you are in doubt.
>
>  Maureen B.

Taking time to pray was very important to people in biblical times, so it should be important to you too. Consider the following examples:

King David: "In the morning, O LORD, you hear my voice; in the morning I lay my requests before you and wait in expectation." —PSALM 5:3

Daniel: "Three times a day he got down on his knees and prayed, giving thanks to his God, just as he had done before." —DANIEL 6:10

The apostle Paul: "Night and day we pray most earnestly that we may see you again and supply what is lacking in your faith." —1 THESSALONIANS 3:10

Jesus: "Very early in the morning, while it was still dark, Jesus got up, left the house and went off to a solitary place, where he prayed." —MARK 1:35

Jesus: "One of those days Jesus went out to a mountainside to pray, and spent the night praying to God." —LUKE 6:12

As you can see from these verses, it doesn't matter what time of day you pray. The important thing is that you do it. But you have to make time. Just like scheduling when you will do homework or when you go to your piano lesson, you need to schedule uninterrupted time for prayer.

Learning to pray regularly is like starting any good habit. It helps to set a regular time every day and stick to that schedule in order for the habit to take hold. Soon it will be so much a part of your life that you'll miss it if you have to skip it!

Jesus' Busy Day

Have you ever thought about the kind of schedule Jesus had? How did He spend His time? What did He do with His free time, or did He have any? When did He pray? The following story, adapted from Mark 6:7–46, gives us insight into a typical day in the life of Jesus and how He spent His time:

Pictures of Prayer

The disciples were so excited as they came back from their mission trip. Jesus had sent them out two by two to the surrounding countryside to tell people to repent and change their ways. By God's power, the disciples did miracles and even cast out

demons. Jesus was full of joy as He heard their enthusiastic reports.

But sad news soon dimmed the joy of the moment. A messenger arrived to tell Jesus that King Herod had beheaded Jesus' cousin John the Baptist. Seeing His tired disciples and feeling His own grief, Jesus tried to get His disciples away for a little break. They got into a boat and traveled to a remote place across the Sea of Galilee.

A crowd of enthusiastic followers recognized them. "Come on," they shouted to their friends. "We can catch them on the other

To be able to spend time with God, you need to carve out time just for Him—no matter how busy or exhausted you are. It might mean getting up a little earlier or getting ready faster in the morning. It might mean giving up a favorite TV show or some computer game time. But God will give you the grace to do it. He wants to be with you! He wants to help you learn to focus your mind and attention on Him. He has so much to share with you!

Reading and Prayer
by Anna, age 11

Prayer Projects

If you love to read (say you read for an hour every night) but sometimes forget to pray, each night after you've finished reading, say your prayers. If you don't know what to pray about, thank God for your friends and family, your love for reading, and all the good things that you can remember that happened that day.

side if we hurry and walk around the lake." When the disciples' boat landed on the opposite shore, the eager crowd was there to greet them.

The disciples must have groaned inwardly at this interruption to their little vacation. But despite His own sorrow and weariness, Jesus felt overwhelmed with compassion for the people. He had already spent the afternoon teaching eager listeners and healing the sick. And now at the close of the day, He miraculously provided a meal of fish and bread for more than five thousand hungry followers. After a day like this, most of us would have

wanted to take a nap or just be alone in our room with no distractions. Not Jesus. He didn't turn the people away. He ministered to their needs.

Then after feeding more than five thousand people (which means it already had been a *very* full day of service and sorrow), Jesus sent His disciples off in the boat while He found a secluded mountainside to pray. No matter how busy He was, no matter how exhausted He was, Jesus *still* found time to pray; or rather, He *made* time to pray.

Need time to pray?

Prayer Projects

Most of us spend about ten minutes in the shower. That's a great amount of time to pray.

Pray in the car or on the bus as you are going to school.

On the way to school, pray instead of listening to the radio or chatting with friends. Focus on what you know will be happening that day, and seek God's wisdom and guidance as the day begins. Maybe a friend will pray with you.

Pray while you are walking the dog.

A walk of any kind is a wonderful opportunity to talk with God and enjoy His creation. Do not let this time go to waste.

Pray during computer "wait" time.

Whether it is waiting for a file to download or waiting for a reply from a friend, why not take that time to pray.

Pray during commercials.

Rather than letting advertisers determine how you spend the time during TV commercial breaks, why don't you set your own agenda by using the time to pray.

Pray while you are cleaning your room or doing other chores.

Instead of wishing you were doing something else, pray!

Praying "Popcorn" Prayers

Prayer times do not have to be long. Small, "bite-sized" prayers can be as valuable and exciting as scheduled prayer times. 1 Thessalonians 5:17 says to pray continually. Always keep in mind that you have God's Spirit living in you. You can have constant and uninterrupted communication at all times. This means you should be ready to pray at any time. If a problem comes up in your life, if you are suddenly very joyful about something, or if a friend asks you to pray for her, you can stop what you are doing and start praying. These are called "popcorn prayers." You can just "pop" a prayer to the Lord at any time and He will be listening! This is one of the great joys of walking in the Spirit.

Prayer on the Go

There are lots of times during your day when you can pray while you are doing something else. Here are some ideas. Can you think of others?

Find a consistent time to pray each day, one that works best for you, but don't make that your *only* time. Talk to God *often* throughout your day.

Prayer Ideas

Dish-Time Prayers
by Jessamine, age 13

When I was visiting my grandmother's house, I offered to wash dishes. As I was alone in the quiet kitchen, I decided to pray while washing the dishes. It is a very convenient time to talk to the Lord, and I enjoyed it so much.

Prayer Bells

Every time you hear a school bell or the phone ring, use it as a reminder to send a quick "popcorn" prayer to the Lord.

Sticky Reminders
by Bethany B.

Post sticky notes on your bathroom mirror of things you need to remember to pray about. You can also leave index cards containing prayer reminders where you will see them: in your Bible, in your backpack, in a back pocket of a car seat, or in your locker.

Joy Ride
by Wendy W. and Sandi S.

Prayer Ideas

This is a fabulous activity that, while you are simply riding in your car, will awaken your senses to many of the great blessings God has provided for you! You will find yourself praying and praising the Lord for His brilliance, creativity, and generosity! It's very easy — all you have to do is open your heart to God and open your eyes to all the wonderful conveniences and beautiful sights around you as you pass by them in your car. You see, it's easy to miss the most obvious blessings in our lives. But this activity will help you tap into God's love for you in a very simple manner.

Here's what you do: **The next time you are riding in the car, look out the window and take notice of everything around you.** Look at houses, stores, signs, roads, sky, trees, etc. Look closely at the businesses and other buildings that you drive past every day but normally don't pay much attention to. Then realize that these things are all God's provision in your life. Thank Him for them, one after another, as you pass by them. God gives us many, many useful, fun, beautiful, and helpful things to enjoy while we live life on this earth!

For instance, the next time you are driving somewhere with your mom, take a look at the scenery around you. What do you pass by? Perhaps you see a bank. Thank the Lord that He holds all the riches under Heaven in His hands, and that He "owns the cattle on a thousand hills." Think about the money God has provided for your family and thank Him for it. Thank Him that He provides banks for safekeeping. Think about the grocery store as you pass by it and thank God for the amazing variety of fresh fruits and vegetables and other groceries He provides for us to choose from. Simply praise God for His good provision for us!

Maybe you pass by a paint store. Think about all the many brilliant shades of colors there are in the world that God created. Thank God for His master artistry that painted the skies blue, the grass and trees green, and the sunsets orange, pink, and red! Thank Him for the blessing of living in a colorful world, rather than a world in all black and white. Also thank Him that we are able to go into a store and actually pick from hundreds of color choices to paint our bedroom or home. This is a simple luxury that we can sometimes forget about, but having a paint store to shop in is a wonderful blessing from God!

What about the hospital you pass by? That is something to be truly thankful for! Thank the Lord for modern medicine and the many doctors and nurses who help the sick. Thank Him for the thousands of different types of medicines that help heal our bodies and make us well. Thank Him that we have clean, safe hospitals and experienced doctors ready to help us any time of day or night. Then remember that the Lord is our Great Physician and Healer of our souls. Praise Him that He forgives your sins and heals your hurts.

We have much to be thankful for, and sometimes it's just a matter of looking out the car window to realize the abundant life and blessings God has given us! Open your heart to God and begin to pray prayers of thanksgiving for all the ways He has enriched your life.

To help you get started, here are a few more things for which to be thankful:

* roads — concrete and asphalt and the intricate road and highway systems that allow us to travel today with ease

    * cars — the means to be mobile

* gas stations — fuel that makes our cars run

    * signs — directions we are given to guide us

* restaurants — many choices of food, plus the ability to be served and not do dishes!

    * trees — shade from the heat, wood for furniture, paper products

* parks — special places to enjoy the beauty of God's creation

    * churches and synagogues — freedom to worship

* schools — readily available education

    * jewelry stores — God deposited gems in the earth for us to find and enjoy

* dry cleaners — places where other people are willing to clean our clothing!

    * print and copy shops — the ability to reproduce words and pictures

* houses — shelters that offer us a sense of safety and security

    * fences — boundaries to keep us and our family pets safe

* fast food places — the convenience of food when we are in a hurry!

    * street lights — the ability to see at night

Can you think of others? Be creative and allow God to open your eyes to the many blessings around you! You will soon turn an ordinary errand into a "joy ride" with the Lord!

Remembering to Pray

People often ask, how can I remember to pray? Many people use visual or audio cues to remind them of what they want to get done. You can do the same thing to remind yourself to pray.

To me praying is telling God how I feel even if I'm not ready to tell others. God cares about what I feel inside even when it seems no one else does. He is always listening!

Emily S., age 11

Prayer Clock
by Mimi B., age 9

Prayer Projects

Collect twelve small pictures of family and friends. Place them in order in the shape of a clock on a large piece of cardboard or poster board. Glue the pictures down. Label the pictures with the numbers one through twelve just like the face of a clock.

Add hands for the clock cut from construction paper, and attach them with a brad through the center of the clock. You can pray on the "hour" for the person at that number or for everybody when you wake up, when you eat, and when you go to sleep. Pray a special prayer if that person is sick or is having problems (friends, family, school, etc.). You can also send cards to each person, letting them know you are praying for them.

Pray everyday

Retreat to a quiet place

Ask Him everything

You're *His* child, so He'll listen to everything you say

Erase all unholy thoughts

Remember He cares about everything

Leah E. R., age 13

A Remember-to-Pray Bookmark
by Alicia P.

Prayer Projects

We want to spend time with God, but sometimes it's hard to remember. Make a bookmark out of poster board or ribbon about one inch by eight inches. Write "Remember to Pray" lengthwise on the bookmark. If you have room, add the words of 1 Thessalonians 5:17, "Pray continually," or another favorite Bible verse. Keep your bookmark in your Bible or other place where you will see it often.

Prayer Ideas

Penny Prayer

Every time you see a penny on the ground, pick it up and say a prayer to the Lord.

Prayer Rock
by Kathleen, age 13

Prayer Projects

This is a rock you put on the floor beside your bed when you go to bed at night, so when you get up the next morning, you step on it and it reminds you to pray. Then when you've finished your prayer, you put it on your pillow, so when you get into bed at night, your head hits it and you remember to say your prayers. Then you put it back on the floor. There is a little rhyme that goes with it:

PRAYER ROCK RHYME
author unknown

I'm your little "prayer rock" and this is what I'll do:
    Just put me on your pillow till the day is nearly through,
Then pull back the covers and climb into bed—
    Whack! Your little "prayer rock" will hit you on the head.
This will remind you as the day is through,
    It's time to say your prayers like you wanted to.
Then, when you are finished, just dump me on the floor
    And I'll stay through the night to give you help once more.
When you get up the next morning, *Clump*, "I stubbed my toe,"
    So you will remember your prayers before you get up and go.
Put me back on your pillow when your bed is all made.
    Your clever little "prayer rock" will remain as your aid.
Because your Heavenly Father cares and loves you so,
    He wants you to remember to talk to Him, you know.

"Remember to Pray" Poem
by Karen S., age 16

Yesterday morning I got out of bed,
Got ready for school, ate my butter and bread,
Said good-bye and started the day
All of the time forgetting to pray.

I got to school with a hole in my skirt,
A ladder in my tights and shoes covered with dirt.
My pen had leaked and my homework had blotted
T'was the math graph I had so carefully plotted.

I went through the day bad-tempered and cross
What had gone wrong? I was completely at a loss
I never once thought of my Father above
Faithfully waiting to administer love.

I got up this morning and knelt down to pray
Today I was determined to start the right way
I went through today with God right by my side
All went okay while I had God as my guide.

Prayer Socks

Prayer Projects

Here are some special socks that you can make to wear when you are walking around at home praying!

Supplies needed:
1 pair of large athletic socks, plain white
1 yard of pre-gathered lace
assorted charms and trims of your choice
4 jingle bells
optional: tie-dye colors of your choice
optional: fabric paint

Leave socks white or dye them a color of your choice. Sew lace around the top edge of the cuff. Trim the cuff with ribbons, bells, and any other charms you choose. (Charms should be symbolic of your faith—a cross, angel, pearl, Bible, etc.) Use fabric paint to write your favorite Scripture verse, the names of God, etc., or to decorate the socks.

You can "prayer walk" around your house! You can also wear your prayer socks when you want to be reminded to pray for something. And you can make prayer socks for your friends!

The sound of the bells jingling on the socks is also a reminder of Old Testament times when bells were sewn onto the edges of the priests' robes. The bells could be heard coming and going from the temple as they ministered before the Lord and interceded for the people. Exodus 39:25 says, "They made bells of pure gold and attached them around the hem between the pomegranates. The bells and pomegranates alternated around the hem of the robe to be worn for ministering, as the Lord commanded Moses."

Chapter 3
Different Ways to Pray

There is not one set style of prayer. People pray in different ways for different reasons. Some people fold their hands, but many others don't. Some people bow their heads, but others look up. Some people close their eyes; others keep them open. Some people pray silently, but others pray out loud. Some people kneel on the floor, but others prefer to sit or stand when they pray. These things don't make your prayers more effective or more likely to be answered, although they may help you center your attention on God.

God sees more than just your physical posture, and He accepts, enjoys, and appreciates any prayer that comes from your heart—regardless of the style in which it is offered. First Samuel 16:7 says, "The LORD does not look at the things man looks at. Man looks at the outward appearance, but the LORD looks at the heart."

Some people think that since they are talking to Almighty God, their prayers should contain fancy phrases or biblical-sounding words such as *thee* and *thou*. They think that if they don't pray in just the right way, God might not hear them. But this isn't true. God wants to hear you pray in your own words. He cares most that you are sincere and honest. He wants you to feel free to tell Him anything, in whatever way is comfortable for you. He wants you to share all your concerns with Him because He cares deeply about you and everything that concerns you. "Cast all your anxiety on him because he cares for you," says 1 Peter 5:7. God wants to hear from you!

God likes the sound of your voice—whether it is the "voice" of your heart or your mouth. A silent prayer and a spoken prayer are equally effective.

If you want to know more about styles of prayer, you can get ideas from some of the prayers in the Bible. Study the Scriptures, and see how people in the Bible expressed themselves to God. Watch for different prayer styles. Turn to Appendix A in the back of this book, "Prayers in the Bible," to get you started.

You might be surprised to see that the Bible records different positions for prayer. Here are just a few examples:

lifting up hands in prayer
(PSALM 28:2; 1 TIMOTHY 2:8)

falling facedown on the ground
(NUMBERS 16:22; 1 CHRONICLES 21:16–17)

standing then kneeling
(2 CHRONICLES 6:12–14)

kneeling
(EZRA 9:5; ACTS 20:36)

lying down
(ISAIAH 38:1–3)

scrunched inside the belly of a big fish
(JONAH 2:1)

Your Prayer Style

Prayer Skills

Everyone has a unique way of praying to God. Prayer is something that is very personal and very adaptable to individual tastes, styles, and circumstances. Look at each of the following options, and decide which ones most often describe how you pray. You might realize that you have used many of these prayer styles. There are no right or wrong answers.

When I pray, I prefer to:

kneel	use many words
sit down	use few words
stand	pray Bible verses
bow my head	include praise songs
close my eyes	pray alone
fold my hands	pray with other people
lie on my stomach with my face to the ground	pray in private
walk around	pray in public
pray out loud	write my prayers down
pray silently, inside my mind	sing my prayers

The position you pray in or the type of words you use are only important
if they help you to better focus on God.

Sing and make music in your heart to the Lord, always giving thanks to God the Father for everything, in the name of our Lord Jesus Christ.

—EPHESIANS 5:19–20

Creative Ways to Pray—Spoken Words Optional

When spoken words aren't quite enough, there are many creative ways to express your feelings and requests to God. You can draw, write, or create a message for or about God—His nature, His actions, or His characteristics—as a form of praise to Him.

Praying Anywhere!

Pictures of Prayer

Prayer is something you can do anywhere, as we will see in this story, adapted from the book of Jonah:

Jonah fell down, down, down into the heaving sea. Already the boat was long gone, hefted away from him by a mighty wave. *This is it*, Jonah thought. *I am going to drown. I am going to die because I disobeyed God's command to go to Nineveh.*

Something dark and sinister came beside him. Was Jonah even aware of the approach of the large fish? So close to death, he probably didn't even care whether he died by drowning or as fish food. With one gulp, darkness engulfed him. Jonah waited for the end of his life.

But it never came. Miraculously he was still alive inside that huge fish. He took a deep breath and another and another. For the moment, he was definitely alive.

I LOVE YOU MORE AND MORE
by Karen S., age 16

The eagles fly above me
The fish swim down below
Your animals around me
Oh how I love You so.

You've given me a garden
And animals galore
A forest full of songbirds
And waves upon a shore.

For the eagles and the fish,
The waves upon the shore,
The garden and the songbirds
I love You more and more.

HELP ME
by Karen S., age 16

Oh Lord I see Your wisdom
In everything around
There's a feeling of security
Where Your arms surround
Lord help me to remember
I'm guided by Your hand
And when others
seem to forget You
Help me, for You,
to stand.

Jonah knew God caused the storm that compelled the sailors to throw him overboard. Jonah knew it was impossible for a man to be swallowed by a fish and still be alive. This was definitely God's hand at work. Jonah also knew he needed to ask God's forgiveness for his disobedience in not preaching God's message in Nineveh.

How does one pray while inside the belly of a fish? We don't know how cramped Jonah was inside the fish. At that moment, however, body position was probably the last thing on his mind. He was just grateful for God's intervention, and he wanted to renew his relationship with God. He wanted to get back on track with God and do what God wanted him to do. So Jonah prayed in the belly of the fish.

Musical Prayers
by Elizabeth H., age 16

Prayer Ideas

My prayer idea is actually a praise idea too. (Praise is a form of prayer to God!) I love to listen to Broadway musicals and big band and swing music. If I listen to a song a lot, I memorize it without even knowing it. Sometimes I replace the words to the songs with my own words. For example, from the musical *The King and I* (a great musical, which everyone should see!), I take the song "Getting to Know You," but I sing it to myself as "Getting to Know *Him*" so that it is a praise song about God.

You can put Bible verses in songs too! For example, you could sing the words of Proverbs 3:5–6 to the tune of a favorite song. The next time you hear that song, try singing your words—telling God how much you love Him! Even if you may think, *I am not a good singer* or *I could never think up lyrics like that,* God doesn't care! He will love anything you do to praise Him. So, use the songs as prayers.

How Jesus Prayed

Prayer was a very important part of Jesus' life, and His disciples could tell. Day after day, they saw Jesus praying—for strength, for wisdom, to heal, to drive off evil spirits, and more. Prayer was a natural part of His life.

Before they met Jesus, the disciples lived under the Old Testament laws. They probably saw God primarily as a lawgiver and not as Someone who took a personal interest in the details of their lives.

Jesus, however, prayed to God in a very intimate manner. The disciples must have longed to talk to God in such a personal way. They said, "Lord, teach us to pray" (Luke 11:1). So Jesus did.

In Luke 11:2–4 and Matthew 6:9–13, Jesus taught His disciples what is called the Lord's Prayer. The passage in Matthew goes like this:

OUR FATHER in heaven, hallowed be your name, your kingdom come, your will be done on earth as it is in heaven. Give us today our daily bread. Forgive us our debts, as we also have forgiven our debtors. And lead us not into temptation, but deliver us from the evil one.

The Lord's Prayer Includes a Number of Different Parts

Our Father in heaven: Acknowledgement that God is our Father. hallowed [holy] be your name: Expression of praise and honor to God. your kingdom come, your will be done on earth as it is in heaven: Petition that God's ways and works will be seen in the earth.

Give us today our daily bread: Prayer for daily needs. Forgive us our debts, as we also have forgiven our debtors: Request for forgiveness from God as we offer forgiveness to others. And lead us not into temptation, but deliver us from the evil one: Prayer for protection from sin and Satan.

Traditionally, this prayer is ended with the following declaration of God's supremacy: "For Yours is the kingdom and the power and the glory forever. Amen."

The Lord's Prayer was not the only way Jesus prayed. He prayed many different ways and in many different circumstances. Some of His prayers were long, such as the prayer found in John 17, which is twenty-six verses long. In that prayer, Jesus prayed for Himself, for His disciples, and for all believers, including you. At other times, Jesus' prayers were short, as in Luke 23:46, when Jesus called out, "Father, into your hands I commit my spirit."

Prayers do not have to be long to be powerful. Even when Jesus prayed what appeared to be

Prayer Projects

Write a song

The book of Psalms is actually a songbook of the songs the Jewish people sang. They are also prayers to God. You can write and sing your own song of prayer to God too.

Write a letter to God
by Diane R. and Lindsey K.

Write a letter to God in your journal as if you are writing to a friend. Start your letter with "Dear God" and sign your name at the end. Keep your letters to God in a folder that you can also decorate. Later, reread your letters. This will be a good record of how your faith in God is growing. You can call your letter file, *My Jesus Journal.*

Draw your prayer requests

If you love to draw, have a sketchbook handy, so you can draw as you pray. The Holy Spirit might bring an image or picture to your mind as you spend time in God's presence.

Personalizing the Lord's Prayer

Prayer Ideas

The Lord's Prayer can be prayed just as it is, or you can use it as a model to create your own prayer. In your own words, write a prayer to God in your prayer journal. Use the following format to give your prayer a structure, but be specific and personal as you pray through each part.

Part 1 Acknowledge that God is your Father **Thank You, God, for being my Daddy.** Part 2 Express praise and honor to God **I exalt and praise You! I love You!** Part 3 Petition that God's ways and works will be seen in the earth **Lord, help my friends at school see Your love and know Your ways.** Part 4 Pray for daily needs **Help my mother get better.** Part 5 Request forgiveness from God as you offer forgiveness to others **Forgive me for my anger today and help me to forgive my brother.** Part 6 Pray for protection from sin and Satan **Protect me while I travel to Grandma's this weekend.**

"small" prayers, they affected the people around Him in great ways. For example, remember when Jesus fed more than 5,000 people with what little bit of food was on hand (five loaves and two fish)? He offered a simple, trusting *prayer of thanksgiving* to His Father. Then, out of that prayer flowed a wonderful miracle—the food was multiplied and everyone had more than enough. Did you ever imagine that a prayer of thanks could be that powerful?

Jesus prayed with other people as well as by Himself. Just before Jesus raised Lazarus from the dead in John 11:38–44, Jesus was standing at the tomb in the midst of a group of people. He looked up and prayed, "Father, I thank you that you have heard me. I knew that you always hear me, but I said this for the benefit of the people standing here, that they may believe that you sent me."

However, in many other instances, Jesus was alone when He prayed:

Very early in the morning, while it was still dark, Jesus got up, left the house and went off to a solitary place, where he prayed. —MARK 1:35

Yet the news about him spread all the more, so that crowds of people came to hear him and to be healed of their sicknesses. But Jesus often withdrew to lonely places and prayed. —LUKE 5:15–16

Jesus probably loved going to the mountains or sitting by the Sea of Galilee, where He could enjoy His Father's creation. He probably had a few special places where He really loved to go. There's nothing like sitting with nature all around you to help you feel closer to the Lord.

Night Watch

David says in Psalm 63:6, "On my bed I remember you; I think of you through the watches of the night." The Hebrews divided the night into segments, or watches, for their soldiers to remain on duty. A watch is a time to be alert and watchful. David stayed up all through these watches, thinking of God and waiting on Him to speak.

Plan a night watch with God. Choose a beautiful starry night, preferably when the moon is not too bright, so you can clearly see the stars. Set up a tent in your backyard or lay your sleeping bag on your back deck and lie under the stars. Plan to do this by yourself, but of course make sure you've asked for your parents' permission. You might want to check with the newspaper to see when a meteor shower is scheduled during the night hours, or you can search on your computer for a web site that charts the lunar calendar. Choose to stay up that night to watch God's glory in the heavens. Have your flashlight, Bible, journal or prayer notebook, and pen available.

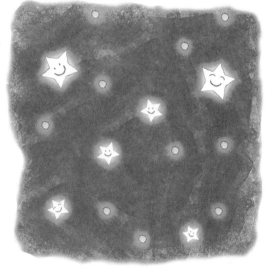

Find a book about the constellations or print some star charts off the computer. Then take it with you and try to locate a few. This is lots of fun! If it is late enough at night or into the fall months, look for the impressive constellation Orion. It is easy to locate, and it's even mentioned in the Bible (Job 9:9). You can also find the Bear mentioned in the same passage (that's the Big Dipper). Pleiades is a star cluster mentioned, which is also easy to find. Lie back and look at those stars! You are looking at stars that civilization has gazed upon for thousands of years. Jesus probably looked at them in the Garden of Gethsemane! Be filled with the wonder of God! Read Psalm 8:3–4, and praise Him for His handiwork in the heavens.

Read the passage about Abraham and his night vigil with God in Genesis 15:1–6. God promised Abraham that He would do the impossible: Abraham did not have even one child, yet God promised He would give this old man descendants more numerous than the stars. Lie back and see if you can count the stars. Can you, as Abraham did, believe and trust God to do impossible things for you? Such faith pleases God! You can't count and name all the stars, but Psalm 147:4 tells us that God does. Lie down and meditate on this wonderful verse. This same God also counts the hairs on your head (Matthew 10:30, Luke 12:7) and is able to do above and beyond what you can imagine (Ephesians 3:20)! Bask in this truth, and let it sink deep into your spirit. Believe Him for your impossible things!

Prayer Ideas

A Secret Meeting

Mark 1:35 says, "Very early in the morning, while it was still dark, Jesus got up, left the house and went off to a solitary place, where he prayed." It was as if Jesus had His own secret meeting places with God.

Set up your own secret meeting place with God. Find a place, preferably outside, away from the noise and the crowds. If you can't find a place outside, find a cozy little spot in your home, like your closet or another secret place to hide where you can't be disturbed. Imagine yourself stealing away to be with Jesus and finding Him there waiting for you. You have so much to share. You and Jesus are definitely kindred spirits! Of course you know He can hear you all the time, but it's fun to have a secret place just for the two of you. Take your journal and your Bible, and have fun.

Sifted as Wheat

In Luke 22:31–32, Jesus predicted that Simon Peter would be tested by Satan. "Simon, Simon," Jesus said, "Satan has asked to sift you as wheat. But I have prayed for you, Simon, that your faith may not fail. And when you have turned back, strengthen your brothers." The test was soon to come, and Simon Peter failed miserably by denying that he knew Jesus three different times. He was bitterly grieved over his weakness, but he held on to the knowledge that Jesus had prayed for him. Because of that, his faith ultimately prevailed.

Is there someone you know who is being tested by Satan right now? You, too, can pray as Jesus did. Pray that this person's faith will not fail. Write a note to let the person know you are praying about the situation.

Praying about Critical Decisions

In Luke 6:12–16, Jesus went out to a mountainside to pray and spent the night praying to God. He had to make a critical decision the next day. He was to choose twelve men to be His disciples. Those twelve men would be vital to His mission of spreading the Gospel and taking care of the church in its infancy. Therefore, they had to be carefully chosen. Jesus spent all night alone on the mountainside praying to God the Father. The next morning, He knew exactly which twelve men to choose.

Is there something for which you really need wisdom? Are you facing a critical decision or a difficult challenge? If so, take a lot of time to pray. Notice what Jesus did. He sat before His Father the whole night. You may not have to stay

Altars of Memorial

Prayer Projects

In Genesis, we often read where the patriarchs would pile stones together to commemorate something important God did for them or promised. This act was another type of prayer. It served to remind the people of what God had said or done. In Genesis 28:18, we see Jacob building an altar at the place where he had a dream from the Lord and God spoke to him great promises. We read in Joshua 4:1–9 that when God parted the waters of the Jordan River for the Israelites to pass to the other side, Joshua took twelve stones (one for each tribe of Israel) from the middle of the river. With those twelve stones, Joshua built an altar of memorial (or remembrance) to God.

Build your own altar of memorial. Have you heard God speak a special promise to you, or has He done something awesome, which you don't want to forget? Build an altar to remind yourself and God of this special and significant time in your walk with Him. When you see your altar, you will be reminded of what God has promised or done and you will be strengthened in your faith. Let it be a special sign between you and God. You don't have to tell others if you want it to be private.

Be creative when making your memorial altar. You can make it as simple as a pile of rocks, or you can plant a little garden, or create a more elaborate memorial using any materials you wish.

up all night, but the point is that sometimes you have to spend a lot of time listening and praying about something before you get the answer.

Jesus was willing to sacrifice sleep to talk to His Father. Prayer was more important to Him than sleep. Prayer is always a sacrifice. You may have to sacrifice some things in order to make time to pray too. Is it worth it to you? If not, be honest with God and ask Him to help you *want* to pray more.

In our prayers, we need to admit to God that while we may want one thing, we are limited in our understanding of what is best for us. We need to give God permission to do what is in our best interest, as Jesus did when He told His Father on the way to the Cross, "May your will be done." (MATTHEW 26:42)

In prayer, you can let out all your wants and needs to the Lord, and He will answer them in His own creative way. Whenever I pray, I think that I am standing in front of God and talking to Him. That way it is so easy! I get so comforted knowing that the Lord, my God, is there with me as I speak to Him. Praying can be so much fun if you let yourself get into it!

Sabrina M., age 10

Prayer Projects

Personal Worship
by Ryanne L., age 14

I believe that as a Christian, you must make God your *top* priority. Personal worship is essential to having a healthy relationship with Jesus. Here is my "formula" for personal worship in hopes that someone might find it helpful.

What you need:

A quiet place—no interruptions allowed

A CD player and a worship CD (optional)

Your Bible and a devotional

An empty notebook

First, choose a time during which you can worship on a daily basis. Then, at that time each day, turn on your worship music and sing along. You might not think that your voice sounds good, but that doesn't matter to God. *All* praise is accepted by Him. You can either turn the music off during this next step or you can keep it on.

After a couple of songs, spend time reading your Bible and doing your devotion for that day. And then, *pray!* I like to make a list of people (here's where the notebook comes in) that I want to pray for and then tell God their prayer needs. Also tell God what's going on in your life—He wants to be a part of it!

You might think that since God knows all, you don't need to confess your sin or tell Him what's going on. But you do! That's (I think) the key to growing closer to God! Do this every day. And when you see one of your prayers answered, write it down by the request! God's blessings on you and your worship!

Chapter 4
Elements of Prayer

In order to help you develop your own unique prayer life, this chapter will explore different elements that you might consider including in your prayers. Prayer is not about formulas. You can create your own ways of expressing yourself to God. The most important thing is that your prayers are from your heart.

Even though there are no set formulas, there are many useful tools to help guide and encourage you as you pray, especially if prayer is something new to you. One such helpful tool is this simple acrostic, which spells *pray*:

Praise

Repent

Ask for Others

Y: Ask for Yourself

Seeing the Elements

Prayer Skills

For this activity you will need your prayer journal (or a piece of paper), a pen or pencil, and a Bible. Look up Psalm 25 and read through it. Write out the Psalm in your journal, and then see how many of the prayer elements you can find—things such as praise to God, repentance (sorrow for sin), asking God to help others, and asking God to help you. Underline each one that you see. You can also look up other prayers in the Bible and do the same thing see (Appendix A) or write your own prayer using the four elements. Remember, each prayer is unique and there is no set formula.

The First Element—Praise

Why Praise God?

Sometimes we get so bogged down by our prayer needs, we forget about all that God has done for us! That's why it is important to start our prayer time with *P* for Praise, the first letter in our acrostic, P.R.A.Y.

When we praise God, we tell Him that we understand He is much greater than any other human being. By thanking Him when we praise, we acknowledge that everything we possess is a result of His goodness to us, not because it's our right to have it. When we fail to praise God and thank Him for what He has done, we begin to take His good gifts for granted. Then when we don't get what we want, we are tempted not to trust that God will provide for us.

Pause for a moment and imagine trading places with your mom. How would you feel if your kids always asked you for things but never showed gratitude when you gave them what they wanted? In fact, what if they got mad when you didn't give them what they wanted or didn't get it to them fast enough? What kind of relationship would you have with such children?

It's the same way in prayer. We need to spend time telling God how wonderful He is and thanking Him for the great things He has done for us. If our prayers only consist of requests, we won't be able to have a close relationship with God. Forgetting to praise Him would make us selfish, ungrateful, and resentful when we didn't get what we wanted.

O LORD, you are my God; I will exalt you and praise your name, for in perfect faithfulness you have done marvelous things, things planned long ago. —ISAIAH 25:1

God wants us to be full of thanksgiving in *everything*. That means in the bad times too. It can be difficult to be thankful when things are going wrong. It might not even make sense. But remember, God is a perfect Father. He really knows what's best for you. When you are sick, your father or mother may give you bad-tasting medicine, which you would rather not take, but you know it's good for you and will help your body heal. Your Heavenly Father wants you to be thankful in bad times because He knows this is best for you and it will bring healing, strength, and renewed hope to your soul and spirit.

Consider it pure joy, my brothers, whenever you face trials of many kinds, because you know that the testing of your faith develops perseverance. Perseverance must finish its work so that you may be mature and complete, not lacking anything. —JAMES 1:2–4

Prayer Ideas

Give Thanks to the Lord

Read through Psalm 136 and then write your own similar Psalm of thankfulness to God. Use the first verse the way it is, and then use your own words and phrases to make up the rest, following a similar pattern. Describe things for which you are thankful, such as things God has helped you with, and then repeat *His love endures forever* after each line. For example,

Give thanks to the Lord, for he is good,
His love endures forever.
To Him who helped me learn to pray,
His love endures forever.
Who by His love gave me a little brother,
His love endures forever.
He gave my dad a brand-new job,
His love endures forever.

Nature's Beauty
by Jaclyn K.

Plant some flowers in a flowerpot. Every time you water your flowers, thank God for the beauty of His earth and the enjoyment His world gives you.

A.C.T.S. Prayer
Submitted by Michelle E., age 12

Prayer Ideas

If you have trouble thinking of what to say in prayer, use this idea. It is called the A.C.T.S. prayer (Adoration, Confession, Thanksgiving, Supplication). Begin your prayer by telling God how much you love Him. Then confess your sins, thank Him for His work in your life, and close with your prayer requests for yourself and others. I use this as my guide, and it really helps me to focus on God!

What do the following verses suggest about praising God?

Do not be anxious about anything, but in everything, by prayer and petition, with thanksgiving, present your requests to God. And the peace of God, which transcends all understanding, will guard your hearts and your minds in Christ Jesus.
— PHILIPPIANS 4:6–7

Be joyful always; pray continually; give thanks in all circumstances, for this is God's will for you in Christ Jesus.
— 1 THESSALONIANS 5:16–18

These verses tell us that there are *always* reasons to thank and praise God—even if we have to search to find them!

Praise for Victory

Have you ever heard of an army fighting a war with **weapons of praise**? When God tells us in His Word to be thankful in all things (see 1 Thessalonians 5:18), He even meant during times of intensity and conflict. Read about King Jehoshaphat's army and how they won a war by praising God (see 2 Chronicles 20:1–29):

Pictures of Prayer

"O King Jehoshaphat," the messenger cried, gasping for breath. "A huge army is on the move toward you. They intend to make war on you!"

Immediately, Jehoshaphat sent an order to his people. He ordered them to start praying and fasting. All of the people of Judah came to the capital city to pray and seek God about what He wanted them to do.

God sent a message to the frightened people through a prophet named Jahaziel. When the Spirit of the Lord came upon Jahaziel, he told everyone, "Don't be frightened or discouraged. You won't even have to fight this battle. Just stand firm and watch how God intends to deliver you from this threat."

Three Good Reasons to Praise God

Praise God for who He is—His character, His personality, and His nature. Learning to praise God this way takes practice. Before you can praise God for who He is, you have to know what He is like. As you grow in your life of faith, you will learn more of what God is like. For starters, see the descriptions of God given in Appendix D.

Praise God for what He gives you. Some gifts He gives every day in normal ways. But they are still gifts from God, and you need to praise Him for those gifts. He gives you other gifts when you ask for them. You can tell they came from Him by the special way you receive them. Some gifts are tangible gifts you can see such as food, shelter, clothes, and friends. Other gifts are unseen, like our faith, the hope of Heaven, and courage when we are afraid.

> Praise is thanking God for the good things He has done and for who He is. As we praise the Lord, we should also be willing to be His servant and to obey Him, because we realize He is our King and Lord of all.
>
> Elizabeth E., age 10

When Jehoshaphat and the people heard this, they fell on the ground and worshiped God. Some people then stood up and praised God. They didn't whisper their praise; they shouted as loud as they could!

The next day, Jehoshaphat and his army set out to meet the warring enemy. Did Jehoshaphat put his best soldiers at the front of the line? No! God had said, "You won't have to fight this battle." Jehoshaphat took God at His word and put a praise band and singers at the front of the line. They marched out to meet the enemy, singing songs of praise!

When they came to the place that overlooked the desert plain, they discovered the dead bodies of their enemies strewn all over the ground. The enemies of Judah started fighting each other and ended up killing each other until no one was left! Jehoshaphat and all the people went back home to hold a huge praise service for the way God had saved them from their enemies.

Praise God for what He has done. Perhaps God helped one of your parents find a job. Perhaps you saw God protect your family in a powerful way. These are things God has done, and you need to remember to praise Him—not once, but over and over again, so you are constantly reminded how powerful He is. Sometimes the things God does are less than obvious, especially if you aren't looking. But God is still working His mighty power in your life, even when you don't see it. It is important to praise Him for this as well.

If you run out of ideas on how to thank God, read some of the Psalms and other praise poems in the Bible (see Appendix C). Psalm 103 is a great place to find things for which to praise God.

Psalm 103 Praise

Prayer Ideas

Write your own psalm, following the pattern of Psalm 103. Use the first two verses as your introduction. Then write your own verses that tell what God has done in your life. Type your praise psalm on a computer in a pretty font, and print it out to hang on your wall or give to a friend.

Joy Box
by Isolyn D.

Prayer Projects

Construct a Joy Box to hold special items that will remind you to praise God. You will need an empty shoebox, gift wrap, stickers, paper, pens or pencils, glue, and scissors. Cover the shoebox with gift wrap, using glue or tape. Cover the lid separately. Write the word *Joy* on the lid. Decorate the box with stickers and Bible verses that talk about praising God. Fill the box with items that reflect the blessings in your life, such as photos of friends and family, pictures of the foods you like, or postcards showing special vacation sites. When you feel down, go through the items in your Joy Box and praise God for His goodness.

A Joyful Noise
by Minga

Prayer Ideas

When I am not feeling connected with God, I sing to Him. The Bible says, "Make a joyful noise unto the Lord," so I do just that. It really gives me peace. You do not have to be a beautiful singer (I am not for sure). All you have to do is make a joyful noise and love Him. Love Him because He first loved you.

Alphabet Thanks
by Ivy H. and Jaclyn K.

Prayer Ideas

This is a fun project to do with friends at a sleepover or with your family in the car. The first person thinks of something to thank God for that starts with the letter **A** and says, "I'm thankful for . . ." The next person repeats what the first person has said, then names something to thank God for starting with the letter **B**. The game continues until you have reached **Z**. Help those who forget only if they ask for it, but don't ridicule those who can't remember. You can also play this game by naming descriptions of God that start with the different letters of the alphabet. (For ideas, see Appendix D, "The Nature and Character of God from A to Z," in the back of this book.)

The Second Element—Repent

Why Repent?

The second letter of our acrostic P.R.A.Y. stands for *Repent*. When we come to God in prayer, we need to admit what we have done wrong and how we have displeased Him. Repenting is not just telling God we are sorry. The word *repent* means to "change our ways and behavior."

In 2 Samuel 12, Nathan confronted King David about having Uriah killed so David could marry Uriah's wife, Bathsheba. Upon hearing Nathan's message, David immediately realized what he had done. In great despair, David said, "I have sinned against the LORD" (v. 13). King David had to repent for his sins, just like we do. And like David, we need to tell God *what* we've done wrong, and *how* we want to change, and ask for His help in changing our lives. Read Psalm 32:1–8:

Blessed is he whose transgressions are forgiven, whose sins are covered. Blessed is the man whose sin the LORD does not count against him and in whose spirit is no deceit. When I kept silent, my bones wasted away through my groaning all day long.

For day and night your hand was heavy upon me; my strength was sapped as in the heat of summer. Then I acknowledged my sin to you and did not cover up my iniquity. I said, "I will confess my transgressions to the LORD"—and you forgave the guilt of my sin.

Therefore let everyone who is godly pray to you while you may be found; surely when the mighty waters rise, they will not reach him. You are my hiding place; you will protect me from trouble and surround me with songs of deliverance. I will instruct you and teach you in the way you should go; I will counsel you and watch over you.

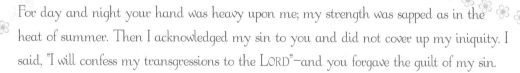

In verses 1–2, David proclaimed that a man whose sins are forgiven and covered by the Lord is truly blessed. He could say this with deep personal conviction because he had tasted the bitterness of unconfessed sin (vv. 3–4). Unconfessed sin robs the body, soul, and spirit of strength and well-being. When David confessed his sin to the Lord (v. 5), he knew—and probably felt—the immediate effects of God's forgiveness. You can hear the restoration of his joy and faith in God in verses 6–7, and in verse 8 we see that his relationship with God had been restored and God could once again guide, instruct, and watch over him.

When we come before God in prayer, we don't want anything to get in the way of our talking to Him as our best friend. We might find a quiet place to pray, away from people. We should also check inside ourselves to see if there are any unresolved conflicts between God and us, for if we have disobeyed God, it will be more difficult to talk with Him.

> If I had cherished sin in my heart, the LORD would not have listened; but God has surely listened and heard my voice in prayer. Praise be to God, who has not rejected my prayer or withheld his love from me!
>
> —PSALM 66:18–20

Imagine that you and your best friend have had a major blowup. Your friend hurt you deeply and betrayed your friendship. Now, imagine that your friend comes to you, asking to borrow something or asking you to do something for her. How would you feel? Would you be a bit indignant that she had the nerve to ask for something without even saying she was sorry?

That is what you are doing when you ask God to answer your prayers without confessing the ways you have disappointed Him. The good news is that God is more than willing to forgive you. As soon as you tell Him you are sorry and you want to change, He will forgive you and help you with your struggles.

> And when you stand praying, if you hold anything against anyone, forgive him, so that your Father in heaven may forgive you your sins."
>
> —MARK 11:25

A Note of Apology

Prayer Projects

To repent is to tell God how sorry you are for your sins—to apologize to Him. To repent also means to turn away from your wrong behavior. We all sin often, so we frequently need to make things right with God. One way you can acknowledge your sins before God and turn away from sinful behavior is to write a letter of apology to God. In your letter, tell God what you have done to hurt Him, and then tell God how sorry you are for your behavior. Ask God to help you turn away from your wrong behavior, and explain to Him that you want to change and make things right.

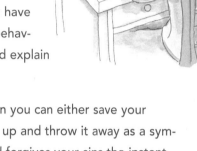

Once you have written your letter, seal it in an envelope. Then you can either save your sealed letter as a reminder of your commitment to God or tear it up and throw it away as a symbol of God's forgiveness being given to you. Remember that God forgives your sins the instant you confess them to Him. "I will forgive their wickedness and will remember their sins no more" (Jeremiah 31:34).

Pebbles of Forgiveness

Prayer Ideas

Find a quite place beside a river or other body of water. Gather several pebbles and put them in your pocket. Think of sins that you want to turn away from and need to ask forgiveness for. For each sin, take a pebble out of your pocket and let it represent that sin. Ask the Lord to forgive you for that sin and help you cast it from your life. Then take that pebble and hurl it as hard as you can into the water.

Read what the writer says in Micah 7:19, "You will again have compassion on us; you will tread our sins underfoot and hurl all our iniquities into the depths of the sea." When you hurl that pebble, you know that you would never be able to find it again, no matter how hard you tried. When God forgives you, it is like that pebble hidden in the depths of the water, never to be remembered again!

Jesus died to pay the penalty of death for the sins we've committed. When we ask for His forgiveness, we can remember that the blood He shed when He gave His life for us covers our sins. When you confess any sin you have committed, He cleans you up so that in His eyes, that black spot of sin and guilt is gone.

> If we confess our sins, he is faithful and just and will forgive us our sins and purify us from all unrighteousness. —1 JOHN 1:9

The Third Element—Ask for Others

The third part of our P.R.A.Y. acrostic stands for *Ask for others*. After you have spent time praising God, confessing your failings to Him, and seeking forgiveness, you are then ready to talk to Him about the needs of the people you would like to pray for. There are so many people who need our prayers!

Often God will bring people to your mind that you need to pray for. When you feel prompted by God's Holy Spirit, send up a "popcorn" prayer for that person. Isn't it awesome that God hears you and cares about everything you care about! No need is too small. He wants you to share *everything* with Him (see 1 Peter 5:7).

The Bible models for us many instances in which people prayed for one another. Consider these verses:

For this reason I kneel before the Father, from whom his whole family in heaven and on earth derives its name. I pray that out of his glorious riches he may strengthen you with power through his Spirit in your inner being, so that Christ may dwell in your hearts through faith. And I

Prayer-List Bookmark
by Lexi, age 13

Prayer Projects

Materials: one piece of colored cardstock paper or poster board, a pen or markers. (1) Take the cardstock or poster board and cut it down to the size of a bookmark, approximately one inch by eight inches. (2) On it write down a list of names of people you need to pray for. (3) Use it as a bookmark (in a reading book or a Bible) so that you will always be reminded to pray for the people on the list. It has really worked great for me, and you should give it a try!

pray that you, being rooted and established in love, may have power, together with all the saints, to grasp how wide and long and high and deep is the love of Christ, and to know this love that surpasses knowledge—that you may be filled to the measure of all the fullness of God.

—EPHESIANS 3:14–19

Is any one of you in trouble? He should pray. Is anyone happy? Let him sing songs of praise. Is any one of you sick? He should call the elders of the church to pray over him and anoint him with oil in the name of the Lord. And the prayer offered in faith will make the sick person well; the Lord will raise him up. If he has sinned, he will be forgiven. Therefore confess your sins to each other and pray for each other so that you may be healed. The prayer of a righteous man is powerful and effective.

—JAMES 5:13–16

Many people tend to pray only for people who are facing tough times or who are sick, but we should also pray for God's blessings on people even when they are not going through difficulties. Consider this prayer from Numbers 6:22–26:

The LORD said to Moses, "Tell Aaron and his sons, 'This is how you are to bless the Israelites. Say to them: "The LORD bless you and keep you; the LORD make his face shine upon you and be gracious to you; the LORD turn his face toward you and give you peace."'"

In addition, we need to remember to pray for those who need our prayers all the time, like our national leaders. In 1 Timothy 2:1–2, we read, "I urge, then, first of all, that requests, prayers, intercession and thanksgiving be made for everyone—for kings and all those in authority, that we may live peaceful and quiet lives in all godliness and holiness."

Praying for Your Nation and Leaders

Prayer Ideas

Regardless of what nation you live in, there are local, state, and national leaders and issues that need your prayers. Why not gather your friends together on a regular basis to pray for your nation and other areas of concern. Before your meeting, you can research the names of your local, state, and national leaders. Find out their areas of influence and responsibilities, and list ways you can pray for them. Ask your parents to give you suggestions on how to focus your prayers.

Here are some examples of things to pray for:

☆ Pray for wisdom and guidance for the president and other leaders at all levels of government—federal, state, county, and city.

☆ Pray for protection of families, marriages, children, and youth.

☆ Pray for safe and strong schools and excellent teachers.

☆ Pray for health and healing for sick people and wisdom for doctors and medical professionals (cures for cancer, heart disease, etc.).

☆ Pray for wisdom and guidance for lawmakers and an effective and honorable legal justice system (Congress, U.S. Supreme Court, state supreme courts, etc.) and protection for law-enforcement officers.

☆ Pray for provision and protection for widows and orphans, single parents, elderly people, and the poor and needy; justice for the oppressed.

☆ Pray for protection of human life; homes for unwanted babies.

☆ Pray for morality in the entertainment and advertising industries.

☆ Pray for wisdom and compassion for church leaders and workers; unity within the body of Christ.

Prayer Ideas

"Prayer for the World" Party

Request that everyone you invite to your party skip a meal before they come. Make sure everyone gets permission from a parent before they do this. Some people may not be able to skip meals for health reasons. Have all your guests agree to spend the time praying instead of eating. This is called fasting.

When your guests arrive for the party, serve them a meal that would be typical in a third-world country. You could serve clear chicken broth and bread or a bowl of rice. After the meal, pray for people in poor countries. Pray especially that they will come to know Jesus as their Savior.

"Pray for Your Missionaries" Party

Choose a missionary you and your friends know. Plan a party to pray for that missionary and the country he or she works in. Perhaps someone from your church is about to go on a short-term mission trip. Ask that person to come to your party too. Serve foods that might be served in the country she is planning to visit. Ask your mom and youth leaders for help in choosing a menu. Keep it simple!

Get brochures on the country, or get information off the Internet. Write or e-mail the missionary beforehand to get information about his or her work. Ask the missionary what you can pray about. After your meal, let each person pray for the missionary. Take pictures, and write a letter together to tell the missionary about your party. You will have a good time, and your missionary friend will be very encouraged to know how you are praying for him or her.

Praying Hands
by Abby

Prayer Ideas

Use your hand to jog your memory of whom to pray for. Put both palms together, like a pair of praying hands. Let each finger remind you of a different group of people to pray for:

Thumb: Pray for those closest to you.

Pointer finger: Pray for those who guide you—teachers, parents, Sunday school teachers, pastors.

Middle finger: Pray for those in high positions—government leaders.

Ring finger: Pray for those who are weak and sick.

Pinkie: Pray for yourself.

Secret Prayer Box
by Tabitha E., age 12

Prayer Projects

If you have problems or prayers you want to keep between you and God, here is a way you can feel like you shared it. Get a shoebox and cut a hole in it for your paper. Write your prayer on your paper. For example, "My friend and I got in a fight and I don't know if I should tell my mom and dad." By putting it in your box, you are sharing it with God.

The Fourth Element— Ask for Yourself

As important as it is to pray for other people, it is also important to pray for yourself. You are important to God, so it isn't selfish to pray for yourself and ask God to meet your needs.

The Prayer of Jabez

> Jabez cried out to the God of Israel, "Oh, that you would bless me and enlarge my territory! Let your hand be with me, and keep me from harm so that I will be free from pain." And God granted his request. —1 CHRONICLES 4:10

It's not selfish to ask other people to pray for you, either. When you ask others to pray for you, you admit that you need God's help to make it through life. It's OK to admit you need help—we ALL do! Even the apostle Paul asked his friends to pray for him.

> Pray also for me, that whenever I open my mouth, words may be given me so that I will fearlessly make known the mystery of the gospel, for which I am an ambassador in chains. Pray that I may declare it fearlessly, as I should.
>
> —EPHESIANS 6:19–20

Nature Praise Walk

Prayer Ideas

Jesus loved nature. He spoke often about the birds, flowers, trees, plants, and sky. You can tell He spent a lot of time in nature reflecting on His Father's goodness. Take a nature hike and look at everything as if you were seeing it for the first time. Pretend you are blind Bartimaeus right after Jesus healed him.

We can easily miss a lot because we take things for granted. Study carefully some blades of grass, a delicate flower, the trees, and insects. Observe the ever-changing clouds in the sky. Listen carefully for the wind whispering through the trees and the birds singing. Walk by a brook and listen to its bubbling song. Listen carefully and try to hear more than you usually do. Close your eyes, and you will be able to focus even more on what you are hearing.

Daily Diary
by Randi B., age 9

Prayer Projects

A great way to have pure fun (without getting distracted!) during prayer is to write your prayers down—especially in *Millie's Daily Diary*. But if you don't have one, any diary will do. You can also look back at your prayers in the years to come and remember your troubles and delights and how you made it through them.

Best Part of the Day

Prayer Ideas

At the end of each day, thank God for the best thing that happened to you that day. Maybe it was a special meal your mom fixed, a meaningful talk with a friend on the phone, or public recognition from a teacher for a job well done on a project. You can make "Best Part of the Day" a family project. Each night before the youngest brother or sister goes to bed, each family member can share his or her best part of the day. Together thank God for His blessings.

Chapter 5
What to Pray About

In our last lesson, we talked about the importance of praying for other people and for ourselves. Now let's talk about *what* we can pray about when we come before God. For instance, how should we pray for national leaders? How should we pray for someone who is sick? What things are important to God?

Remember this essential point: If it is worth worrying about, it is worth praying about. Philippians 4:6–7 says,

> Do not be anxious about anything, but in everything, by prayer and petition, with thanksgiving, present your requests to God. And the peace of God, which transcends all understanding, will guard your hearts and your minds in Christ Jesus.

Brainstorming with God

Prayer Skills

You may not think you have much to pray about, but you do! Here is an exercise that will help show you just how many things there are to pray about. Go before the Lord with your prayer journal and a pen or pencil. Choose a person to pray for. Then ask the Holy Spirit, your Helper, to bring to your mind specific things that you can pray for. Sit quietly and wait for God to speak. If any thoughts come to you, jot them down.

If nothing comes, then ask yourself, *What is going on in this person's life?* What is happening at his or her school or job? Does the person have family needs? Is there anything emotionally that he or she is struggling with right now? Does this individual need to know Jesus as Savior or just know Him better? Use these questions to springboard you into prayer for your friend or loved one. Take your time with this exercise—the way you would want someone to take time praying for you! God can really use your prayers to touch the lives of others. What a privilege!

If you are concerned about something, pray about it! If you feel stressed over something, pray about it! If you can't get a thought out of your head, pray about it! Remember, 1 Peter 5:7 says, "Cast all your anxiety on him because he cares for you."

Remember also that prayer is not something you must figure out on your own. You have a Helper, the Holy Spirit. (Refer again to the section entitled "The Help of the Holy Spirit" in Chapter 1.) You can trust that the Holy Spirit will help you know what to pray. This is His purpose. Ask Him to lead and guide you in your prayers. He will help you know what to say.

The apostle Paul prayed often for the people in the churches he helped start. Many times he recorded his prayers in the letters he wrote to the churches. Here are some of the prayers he prayed:

Romans
1:10 Paul prayed
that the way might
be opened, so he
could visit his
friends.

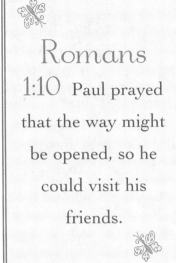

Ephesians
3:16 Paul
prayed that God
would strengthen
them with power
through His
Spirit.

2 Thessalonians 1:11
Paul prayed that God would fulfill
every good purpose and every act
prompted by their faith.

Philippians 1:9
Paul prayed that their
love would abound more
and more.

1 Corinthians
1:4-5 Paul thanked
God for enriching them
in every way.

Prayer Letters

Prayer Projects

Read the following passage from Ephesians. These are portions of Paul's letter to his friends in the city of Ephesus. Gather together some beautiful stationery and colored pens, and write your own letter to a friend or family member. You can even e-mail your letter, using a nice background and pretty font. You can pattern your letter after what Paul wrote to his friends.

EPHESIANS 1:15–19

For this reason, ever since I heard about your faith in the Lord Jesus and your love for all the saints, I have not stopped giving thanks for you, remembering you in my prayers. I keep asking that the God of our Lord Jesus Christ, the glorious Father, may give you the Spirit of wisdom and revelation, so that you may know him better. I pray also that the eyes of your heart may be enlightened in order that you may know the hope to which he has called you, the riches of his glorious inheritance in the saints, and his incomparably great power for us who believe.

Paul's Prayer for the Ephesian Church

Paul was such a loyal friend! He often thought about the people in the many churches he was involved with, wondering how they were doing and faithfully praying for them, even when he was in prison. Although he might not have known everything going on in their lives, he still wrote them letters of encouragement, and he still spent time supporting them in prayer. Read the following example taken from Ephesians 1:15–23 and Ephesians 3:14–21:

Pictures of Prayer

Paul sat in his prison cell. His personal scribe sat across from him, stylus in hand, parchment lying between them. The scribe waited to write the words Paul would speak.

But Paul remained silent, lost in his thoughts. His letter was to be for the church in the city of Ephesus, a church where Paul worked for more than two years. Oh, how he wished he could see them again! There was so much he wanted to tell them about their lives of faith. He wanted them to know that he prayed for

Be Specific When You Pray

When you pray, you can pray very specifically. Paul said exactly what he wanted for the Ephesians in their spiritual growth. Instead of saying, "I pray for my friend who is sick," you can pray, "Give the doctors wisdom to find out what is wrong with my friend. Provide her family with the money to pay the doctor bills."

Instead of praying, "Bless the president," you can pray, "Being president must be a hard job. Give our president energy to do all the jobs he has to do today, and help him stay healthy." Instead of praying, "Bless all the missionaries," you can pray, "Lord, please strengthen Pastor Steve and his family, who are serving in Lithuania. Allow them to build strong relationships with the local people, bringing many to the knowledge of Christ."

Pray in the Spirit on all occasions with all kinds of prayers and requests. With this in mind, be alert and always keep on praying for all the saints. —EPHESIANS 6:18

them often. Paul wanted the new Christians to know what he prayed for, so it would strengthen their faith. When they saw their lives of faith growing, they would know it was happening in part because Paul was praying that God would work in their lives.

"Write this," Paul told his scribe. *"For this reason, ever since I heard about your faith in the Lord Jesus and your love for all the saints, I have not stopped giving thanks for you, remembering you in my prayers...."* Paul told his friends he prayed that they might know Jesus better, that they might understand the hope God gives each believer, and that they might realize what wonderful riches God had for each of them. He prayed that God would help them know how amazing His love is and how this love was available to make a difference in their lives.

The scribe wrote furiously, trying to catch every word of Paul's heartfelt prayer for his special friends.

Parent Prayer

Prayer Ideas

Do you pray for your parents? Guess what? They need prayer too! Parenting is hard work. Parents have stressful lives too, and when they are facing pressure, it's hard to make good decisions. Make a list of different petitions you can pray for your parents. Then go before the Lord on their behalf.

Prayer Montage

Prayer Projects

A montage is a collection of pictures that relate to each other, drawn or pasted onto a larger background. Make a montage of the things you usually pray about. First, write a list of these things, then draw or cut out pictures representing them. Photos and pictures cut from magazines are good sources. Next glue these images onto a piece of poster board or construction paper, and hang the montage in a place where you will be reminded to pray about these people and situations.

Praying detailed, direct, and specific prayers for people helps you to recognize God's answers. If you have prayed that God would help your friend's family with the medical bills from the illness and you hear how her family received a surprise check in the mail, you recognize that God is helping them pay the medical bills.

You can pray for people's spiritual well-being as well as their physical needs. It's fine to pray for physical things like food, success on a test, or even that your team will win a game. But the most important goal in life is growing to love Jesus more and helping others learn about His love. Your prayers for other people ought to reflect these goals.

Sometimes it is hard to know how to pray for people. You can find out by asking someone who knows them well what their needs are. When someone asks you to pray for them, ask, *"How* can I pray for you?" or *"What specifically* can I pray for?" Write down their responses in your prayer journal, then bring the request before God in your prayers.

Prayer Ideas

Prayer Walks
by Abigail N., age 13

This, I believe, is one of the best ways to pray to God. Remember how Aunt Wealthy always went on her "prayer walks" every day, rain or snow? How she was always talking to God on those walks as if He was right there beside her? This is what I do! Since I live in the country, there are a lot of places, such as fields and woods, where I can (finally) have some privacy away from my annoying siblings and the never-stopping racket of the house. I love going on LONG walks, and while I am on those walks, I pray to God. Sometimes I quote Scripture as a prayer, sing praises to God, or just pour out my heart—including my requests. Whether a really big problem or one so small they seem silly! It is really effective! For a while I found it hard to focus on the Lord. My siblings were always bursting into my bedroom, asking me to watch TV (which I really do not care for anyways), saying we are going somewhere, etc., etc. — right in the middle of my private time with Jesus! But while I am gone on a walk, there is nothing to bother me except the birds, deer, and trees (my dog too, but she is okay!). And I love nature, for within it there is the power of God shining! If you live in the city, then what I suggest is to ask God to help you get some privacy. He knows your every talk with Him should be private, so He will help you!

What to Pray on Your Prayer Walk

Take a walk around your home, neighborhood, church, or school. Think about what each room, area, or location represents. For instance, if you're in a house, think about the people who spend time in that particular room, what happens in that room, what the room is used for, and what people come to mind. Whenever people, activities, or events come to your mind, stop and pray for those things. First, thank God for the people that belong in that place and for how God has used those people in your life. Then pray that:

> God would be glorified in all that happens in that room or house.
> God would overcome any evil that is happening in that place.
> God would help these people have a deeper relationship with Him.

If you are having trouble thinking of words, you can always start by reading aloud the following prayers from the Scriptures and then praying them in your own words with *your* Christian friends in mind:

PHILIPPIANS 1:3–6, 9–11

I thank my God every time I remember you. In all my prayers for all of you, I always pray with joy because of your partnership in the gospel from the first day until now, being confident of this, that he who began a good work in you will carry it on to completion until the day of Christ Jesus.... And this is my prayer: that your love may abound more and more in knowledge and depth of insight, so that you may be able to discern what is best and may be pure and blameless until the day of Christ, filled with the fruit of righteousness that comes through Jesus Christ—to the glory and praise of God.

Prayer in a Box
by Kaitlin O.

Prayer Projects

This project is useful when you can't think of anything to pray about. Decorate an old shoebox. Insert dividers to make sections. The dividers can be cut out of index cards or old file folders. Label the sections with these categories or choose categories of your own:

Personal/Family Needs
My Walk with Christ
Relationships with Friends
Those Who Need Salvation
Those Who Are Sick or in Crisis
World Events
Answered Prayer

Write individual prayer requests on slips of paper, and put them in the correct category. When you want to pray, select a slip, pray for the situation, and then put it back in the box. When God has answered a particular prayer, move it to the "answered prayer" section. Take time to select slips from the answered-prayer section and thank God for His answers.

COLOSSIANS 1:3–6, 9–14

We always thank God, the Father of our Lord Jesus Christ, when we pray for you, because we have heard of your faith in Christ Jesus and of the love you have for all the saints—the faith and love that spring from the hope that is stored up for you in heaven and that you have already heard about in the word of truth, the gospel that has come to you. All over the world this gospel is bearing fruit and growing, just as it has been doing among you since the day you heard it and understood God's grace in all its truth.... For this reason, since the day we heard about you, we have not stopped praying for you and asking God to fill you with the knowledge of his will through all spiritual wisdom and understanding. And we pray this in order that you may live a life worthy of the Lord and may please him in every way: bearing fruit in every good work, growing in the knowledge of God, being strengthened with all power according to his glorious might so that you may have great endurance and patience, and joyfully giving thanks to the Father, who has qualified you to share in the inheritance of the saints in the kingdom of light. For he has rescued us from the dominion of darkness and brought us into the kingdom of the Son he loves, in whom we have redemption, the forgiveness of sins.

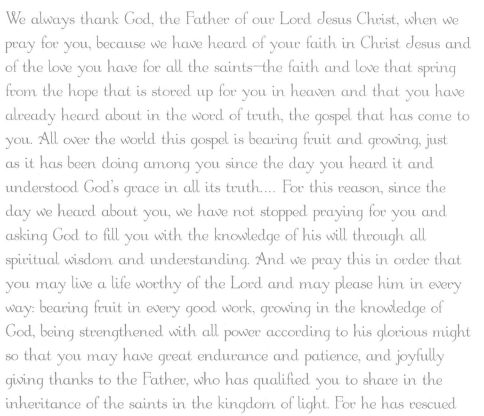

Seven-Up Prayer

Prayer Ideas

If you are just starting to have a daily quiet time and find it difficult to stay focused, here is a method that might keep you on target. Use a kitchen timer at first, but don't be a slave to it. If you are deep into prayer or God leads you to dig deeper into the Bible, forget about the timer!

1 minute: Thank God for the privilege of talking to Him in prayer. Ask Him to help you understand what you read in the Bible today.

1 minute: Read a selected passage in the Bible.

1 minute: Praise God for some part of His character.

1 minute: Repent of anything you have done wrong. If you can't think of anything, admit to God that you are in need of His grace and forgiveness.

1 minute: Be silent. Let God speak to you.

1 minute: Thank God for things He has done or given you.

1 minute: Pray for other people.

ABCs
by Polly, age 13

Prayer Projects

You can pray through the ABCs! Just write down the alphabet on a piece of paper, keeping a generous amount of space in between the letters. After each letter, write down things that start with that letter. Then you can either thank God for the things or pray about them. For example, for the letter A, you might say, "Thank You, Lord, for apples," or you might pray, "Help me with my attitude." You need to keep two papers: one for requests and one for thank you's. You can even keep the pages if you want to and put more things on and take some things off!

Thirty-One Days of Prayer

Prayer Projects

Make a list of the things or people you want to pray for. Try to come up with thirty-one different people, groups of people, or situations. Starting with the first day of a new month, pray for the first thing on your list. The next day, pray about number two, and so on until you reach the end of the month and the end of your list. Here are some ideas you can include on your list:

Teachers	National leaders
Family members	Missionaries
Sunday school	Your future
Your Pastor	An unsaved friend

Change your list at the end of each month, removing the requests that have been answered and adding new things to pray about.

Wedding Prayers

Prayer Ideas

Jeremiah 29:11 says that God knows the plans He has for you. Marriage might be a part of His plan. You may not know if or who you will marry someday, if indeed God plans for you to marry, but God does know. You can start now to pray for your future and possible future husband. Here are some specific things you can pray about:

❀ Ask God to make His plans known to you, and trust Him with your future—even your romantic future.

❀ Pray that God would grant you an undivided heart in your relationship with Him.

❀ Ask God to lead you into a God-honoring relationship, in His perfect timing, if indeed marriage is in your future.

❀ If your future husband isn't a Christian yet, pray that he will become one before you meet him.

❀ You can pray that your future husband will keep himself pure for you.

❀ Pray that God will help you become the kind of woman that will encourage and support your husband in his walk with God.

Chapter 6
Your Friendship with God

Good friends can be hard to come by, but there are few treasures in the world as valuable as a best friend. Pause for a moment and think about the friends you cherish. What is it about those friends that make them so special to you? A good friend is trustworthy. She is someone who really listens when you share a problem or a triumph. She is eager to "get into your world" and know you better.

Likewise, *being* a good friend is also to be valued highly. What characteristics do *you* possess that make you a good friend? Being a good friend means that *you* are trustworthy. You take time to listen, making sure you are not doing all the talking. You are eager to get to know your friend better, asking her questions and learning her interests, not just sharing your own. As you can see, friendship is a *give-and-take* relationship. And to be successful in your friendships, there must be two-way communication.

Give and Take

Prayer Skills

Have a conversation with a friend, but only one of you can do all the talking for three minutes. The other person must try to say something, but the "talker" should continually cut her off. After three minutes, trade places. When the second talker's turn is over, discuss how it felt to be the "listener," unable to share in the conversation.

Listening for God

Spend a quiet moment with God. First, praise Him, thanking Him for what He has done in your life recently. Tell Him you are sorry for wrong things you have done. Read a few verses of the Bible. Then get ready to listen. Tell God, "Speak, Lord, for your servant is listening," as Samuel did in 1 Samuel 3:9. Sit quietly for five minutes. After five minutes, write down the thoughts and the Bible verses that come to your mind.

You might not hear an audible voice like Samuel did, but you will probably have thoughts enter your mind. As you grow in your life of faith, some of these thoughts will be strong impressions that won't go away. That is a good sign that the Lord is talking to you. In your prayer journal, write down your own testimony of how you have heard the voice of God. Take notes on the many ways God speaks to you.

Well, things are no different in your relationship with God. He desires to be your closest, most treasured friend. When you have a deep friendship and fellowship with God the Father, you in turn become an incredible friend to others.

> The scripture was fulfilled that says, "Abraham believed God, and it was credited to him as righteousness," and he was called God's friend.
> —JAMES 2:23

> The LORD would speak to Moses face to face, as a man speaks with his friend. —EXODUS 33:11

(Jesus said,) "Greater love has no one than this, that he lay down his life for his friends. You are my friends if you do what I command. I no longer call you servants, because a servant does not know his master's business. Instead, I have called you friends." —JOHN 15:13–15

This chapter is designed to help you develop your friendship with God. He wants to call you friend and enjoy a relationship with you. But all relationships take work, time, and especially *communication*. You communicate with God through your prayers and through your actions and attitudes. He communicates with you through His Word and the voice of His Spirit deep inside you.

>
>
> Prayer is talking to God like a friend. When you talk to God, He listens to you as you listen to Him. As you get to know God, then you will have a really good relationship!
>
> Maria E., age 8

Friendship with God Requires Humility

You might be thinking, *Humility? What does that have to do with my friendship with God?* Approaching God with humility simply means that you are keenly aware that without Christ you are lost and hopeless, so you are submitted to Him. Yet there is much room to express your feelings with Him. Tell Him when you are angry and disappointed—even at Him. He already knows and He understands. He will not reject you or get angry back. He knows your heart is His. (Read some of the Psalms where David offers complaints to God.) Our hearts don't always yield to the hard things of life immediately. Sometimes it's a process which can take years, until we are finally able to accept, surrender, and move on.

Your righteousness (or goodness) does not come from doing good things, like the Pharisee thought in the story below. Instead, you are made righteous by believing that Jesus died on your behalf, allowing you to have friendship with God the Father. This is called Christ's atoning sacrifice. That is why your attitude before God must be one of deep appreciation and humility, knowing that only the blood of Jesus makes you worthy.

Jesus is looking at your heart. He really wants you to be who you are—simple, real, and genuine—the same way you would want your best friend to communicate with you!

Remember, prayer is getting to know God personally and building an enduring friendship with Him. Prayer is conversation with God. Approach Him with humility, and He will gladly listen. Aren't you excited about a deep friendship with God?

God Hears the Humble

God knows **why** you are praying. He sees into the motives of your heart. If you pray to show off to others or to impress God, it is an ineffective prayer. If you pray only to satisfy your own selfish motives, God is not pleased. Sincerity and humility are the qualities God values most when He listens to your prayers. That's why it is important to remain humble in your relationship with Him. Listen to how Jesus addressed this issue, using two contrasting prayers:

Pictures of Prayer

Luke 18:9–14

To some who were confident of their own righteousness and looked down on everybody else, Jesus told this parable: "Two men went up to the temple to pray, one a

Pharisee and the other a tax collector. The Pharisee stood up and prayed about himself: *'God, I thank you that I am not like other men—robbers, evildoers, adulterers—or even like this tax collector. I fast twice a week and give a tenth of all I get.'*

"But the tax collector stood at a distance. He would not even look up to heaven, but beat his breast and said, *'God, have mercy on me, a sinner.'*

"I tell you that this man, rather than the other, went home justified before God. For everyone who exalts himself will be humbled, and he who humbles himself will be exalted."

A True and Faithful Heart
by Andrea T., age 12

JAMES 5:13–18 Is any one of you in trouble? He should pray. Is anyone happy? Let him sing songs of praise. Is any one of you sick? He should call the elders of the church to pray over him and anoint him with oil in the name of the Lord. And the prayer offered in faith will make the sick person well; the Lord will raise him up. If he has sinned, he will be forgiven. Therefore confess your sins to each other and pray for each other so that you may be healed. The prayer of a righteous man is powerful and effective.

Elijah was a man just like us. He prayed earnestly that it would not rain, and it did not rain on the land for three and a half years. Again he prayed, and the heavens gave rain, and the earth produced its crops.

Prayer is a powerful thing. James told us that Elijah was a man like us who prayed *earnestly* that it would not rain, and it did not rain for three and a half years. The word *earnestly* is the key in this text. In 1 Corinthians 13:2, it talks about having enough faith to remove mountains. When we pray, we must have faith and believe that God can answer our prayers.

But we as Christians can't take for granted God's ability to do all things. In Matthew 21:22 it says, "If you believe, you will receive whatever you ask for in prayer," but the Bible also tells us not to pray with a greedy or selfish motive. Listen to the prayers of the following two men and see how they contrast. First we will listen to Will B. Humble's prayer.

"Lord, forgive me the sins that I have committed against You today. More than once my mind has betrayed You with its thoughts. And Lord, I pray for Mara Anderson, who has the flu, and I know that if it is Your will she will get well soon, for You can do all things. Amen."

Now let's listen to the prayer of I. M. Greedy, Will B. Humble's next-door neighbor. "Lord, I thank You that I am not stupid like Will B. Humble. And I thank You that I am not sick like Mara Anderson. Lord, bless me with health and happiness, for I have served You. Amen."

Which prayer do you think God would be more willing to answer? Will B. Humble's prayer. Will B. Humble believed that God hears and answers prayer, so he prayed continually (see 1 Thessalonians 5:17), and in a few days Mara was well. Notice how Will B. Humble said that if it was God's will for Mara to get better, she would.

When we pray we must keep in mind that our prayers will not always be answered in the way we want them to, but God is wiser and knows what is best for us *always*. We *must pray* continually and in all circumstances. In James 5:13 it says, "Is any one of you in trouble? He should pray. Is anyone happy? Let him sing songs of praise." We should pray about little things and big things, from our neighbor's missing cat to those who have lost loved ones.

When we pray we need to be careful to guard against wanting to look like a godly person to impress others.

Matthew 6:5–8 says, When you pray, do not be like the hypocrites, for they love to pray standing in the synagogues and on the street corners to be seen by men. I tell you the truth, they have received their reward in full. But when you pray, go into your room, close the door and pray to your Father, who is unseen. Then your Father, who sees what is done in secret, will reward you. And when you pray, do not keep on babbling like pagans, for they think they will be heard because of their many words. Do not be like them, for your Father knows what you need before you ask him.

We must pray from a true and faithful heart.

There are many ways that James 5:13–18 applies to us. It's important to pray in every circumstance. But why do we pray in every circumstance?

There are two reasons: ONE, simply because our Lord Jesus commands us to! SECOND, because by praying in every circumstance, we draw closer to our blessed Savior. When our prayer is answered, our faith grows and we have more trust in God. So when you go about the day, think of all the many things you can do with one small prayer.

Friendship with God Requires Your Interest

There's nothing like a friend who shows interest in your life—a friend who wants to know your thoughts, likes and dislikes, style, beliefs, and preferences. It is always enjoyable to share your tastes with a good friend. Likewise, getting to know what makes your best friend tick is a lot of fun too!

But in order to get into the heart of a friend, you must ask questions. You must interact with your friends by listening and pursuing time with them. You must show your friends that you are *interested* in knowing them. A friend would not be a real friend is she didn't show an interest in your life. What if your best friend never asked you questions about yourself? What if she rarely spent time with you? She wouldn't know you very well, and that wouldn't be much of a friendship.

Just as we must pursue our friends and interact with them by asking questions and listening, we must do the same in our friendship with God. Remember, relationships are a matter of give and take.

God is GOD! You aren't! But He wants to spend time with YOU! How cool is that? How can we ignore Him? Speak to Him! Everyone gets bored sometimes. USE THE BOREDOM! But when you start to say, "I'm bored," STOP! Instead of being bored, spend time with God. Study the Word. Pray. He KNOWS when you want to be close to Him. If you stop and listen, He'll speak.

Jessi D., age 13

We have to show God that we are interested in knowing Him. We need to have an eagerness to spend time with Him. How? The most important way we can interact with God is to open up His Word.

Prayer Projects
Faith Binder
by Esther B.

Use a three-ring binder filled with notebook paper to write down especially meaningful verses you find during your devotional time. Write them in a fancy script like Millie might have used. Talk to God about the verses, and have fun getting to know Him through His Word.

Shoe-Box Scriptures
by Lindsey K.

Decorate a shoe box any way you like. Cut a hole in the lid, large enough for your hand to fit through. Write memorable or favorite Bible verses on small slips of paper and store them inside the shoe box. Each morning, select a verse randomly without looking. Try to memorize the verse. Think about the verse all day, thinking about each phrase, what it means, and how you can apply it to your life. Turn the verse into a prayer to God, and ask for His help in applying it. If you succeed in memorizing the verse by the end of the day, don't put that verse back in the box, but rather keep it in a separate box for later review. If you didn't get it memorized, return the slip to the box to work on again another day.

Your Bible is the key to having a two-way conversation with God. You must read the Bible to find out about Him. You will discover God's thoughts, likes and dislikes, personality, and preferences when you read your Bible. After all, you can't have a relationship with someone you don't know very well. God speaks to you through His Word. He will reveal things about Himself that will make your friendship grow much deeper.

God uses His Word to speak to you in other ways. For instance, you might be praying and a Scripture will pop into your mind. God is using the Scripture to speak to you. This can happen even when you are not praying. Your thoughts may turn to a passage of Scripture while you are simply going about your day. Remember, prayer can happen anywhere, anytime. As you faithfully read your Bible, God will show His faithfulness to you—you will get better at hearing Him speak to you. As you become more familiar with the Scriptures, you can pray them back to God and have a conversation with Him about the verses, just like you would discuss an opinion or issue with a friend.

You can also turn God's commands into prayers that ask God to help you obey them. Here is an example:

Bible verses:

> My command is this: Love each other
> as I have loved you. —JOHN 15:12

> Be kind and compassionate to one
> another, forgiving each other, just
> as in Christ God forgave you.
> —EPHESIANS 4:32

Your Prayer:

> "Lord, help me to love my little brother as
> You have loved me, and to be more kind
> and compassionate to him. I choose to for-
> give him for tearing up my book today."

By using the Bible in your prayers:

You can tell God that you are confident He will answer your prayer because of the promises He has made in His Word. You can ask God to help you obey what you have just read in your Bible study. You can thank God that His promises are meant for you.

Prayer Projects

Christian-Walk Cards
by Cora L.

Whenever you find a Bible verse that is helpful to you in your walk of faith, write it on an index card. You can decorate the card with colored markers, but make sure you can read the verse. You can also type the verse in a pretty font on a computer and print it out on a color inkjet printer. Tape the verse where you can see it. When you see the verse, think about how it helps you live your life of faith. Then pray, asking God to help you obey that verse, or thank Him for what the verse shows you about His character.

Hiding the Word in Your Heart

Philippians 4:6–7 and 1 Peter 5:7 are very important verses in the Bible about prayer. Choose one of the verses and write it on an index card. Work at memorizing it. Say it every day, several times a day, for two weeks. Ask family members or friends to test you.

Personalizing Scripture

Replace the pronouns (I, we, you, me) in a passage of Scripture with your name. For example, if Millie were personalizing Philippians 4:19, she would write, "Millie's God will meet all Millie's needs according to His glorious riches in Christ Jesus." Then turn the verse into a prayer like this: "Thank You, God, that You have promised to meet all my needs according to Your glorious riches in Christ Jesus. Because You have promised to meet all my needs, I know that You will take care of me and that I can confidently share my needs with You, knowing that You will keep Your promise to me."

Psalm 121 is a good Psalm with which you can personalize God's promises as a prayer. As you read the following Psalm, mentally take out the personal pronouns, and replace them with your own name. This personalizes the Psalm between you and God. Try reading it out loud.

I lift up my eyes to the hills—
where does my help come from?
My help comes from the LORD,
the Maker of heaven and earth.
He will not let your foot slip—
he who watches over you will not slumber;
indeed, he who watches over Israel
will neither slumber nor sleep.
The LORD watches over you—
the LORD is your shade at your right hand;
the sun will not harm you by day,
nor the moon by night.
The LORD will keep you from all harm—
he will watch over your life;
the LORD will watch over your coming and going
both now and forevermore.

Now, repeat the same activity, only this time change the words so you are saying them directly to God. We'll get you started: "I lift up my eyes to the hills—where does my help come from? My help comes from You, Lord, for You are the Maker of heaven and earth."

You can write your own psalm that expresses your greatest joy or your deepest sorrow. Write the psalm in a beautiful script on homemade stationery or design one on your computer. Here are some psalms by *A Life of Faith* club members:

As the Moon Melts Away
by Cherise L.

As the moon melts away
I'll lift my voice and pray.
In the dawn of the day
I will seek You.

You supply my strength
You provide my peace.
You set my heart on fire with burning desire
To know You more!

I wouldn't trade these moments
If it would make me a king.
I wouldn't trade these moments
For anything!

Come what may
Through my day,
You're by my side.
I so long to abide
In You alone.

So I start my day
In this wonderful way
So You can direct me
So You can instruct me.

I will listen,
I will pray,
At the dawn of each day.
Yes, as the moon melts away, I will seek You.

Loving Eyes
by Sierra N.

Oh Lord, You know me
and You love me.
You watch over me with loving eyes.
I respect and love You
as You guide me through grassy plains and over rocky hills.
You are a wondrous friend,
to whom I trust my secrets.
Lord, You protect me
and take care of me always.
You help me through troubled times.
You are like a post
and I am a vine that can't be pulled away, oh, Lord.

I Love You, Lord
by Cora L.

I love You, Lord, for You are good.
You are there when I need You.
You have given me everlasting life
and protected me from Satan.
You sent Your Son to die for sinners like me.
You are my faithful Friend.
You made the world for me to live in
until You come back to take me to Heaven.
You have given me everything I need
until I'm in Heaven with You.
You have given me friends
when I have needed them.
You are helping me hide Your Word in my heart.
You make every day a cheerful day.
Oh Lord, I love You,
for You are so good to me.

Prayer Projects

Scripture Prayers on Spiral-Bound Note Cards
by Emily L.

Write verses on spiral-bound note cards. Keep your collection in a seat pocket in your family's car. While you are riding in the car, pray those verses to God.

Quiet Time
by Alyssa W.

Read a couple of verses in your Bible. Write a letter to God in your journal, telling Him how you feel about what you have read or what you believe His Word is saying to you. After you have finished writing, ask God in prayer to help you obey what you have read.

When God Calls, Be Ready
by McCall W., age 12

One day after finishing my everyday, go-through-the-motions quiet time, I began to pray a prayer. Then I realized what I was doing. God loved me and died for me and was listening carefully to everything I prayed, but I wasn't even stopping long enough to listen to Him. I was just reading my chapter, asking Him to bless my family and me, and then I was done. That was just another thing to check off my list. Then it hit me. God never checks us off His list after He listens to our prayers. He commits to us 24/7.

I realized that God was calling me to do something so simple: listen. That was all. He only wanted me to listen. I did and He revealed sins to me that I had not even recognized. That day God helped me to see how much He cares. I rededicated my life to Him, and I was extremely blessed. This only happened because when God spoke, I decided to listen. So be ready! If you are open to God's will, He will speak.

Two-Way Prayer
by Maryssa C., age 12

Prayer Ideas

I think prayer is a very special time to talk with God and tell Him what is going on in your life. And I also think it's good to express your feelings and not be embarrassed by them. Prayer is also important because it is like a telephone line between God and you. You can tell Him anything and everything that is going on in your life.

Before you go to bed, talk to God in your room when no one is around, and then you don't have to feel pressured into talking to Him in front of your parents and family. Another thing I have done is to go to a corner away from everyone else and ask God to talk to me. Then I write down the thoughts I have. It is a really good way to listen to God and what He has to say instead of me giving Him a to-do list. This will make prayer more meaningful by having a two-way conversation rather than a one-sided conversation. This way God can talk to you in any way He wants!

Friendship with God Requires You to Listen

It's so nice when a friend listens quietly as you share what's on your mind, isn't it? And when that friend offers a word of support and understanding in response, you feel loved, supported, and encouraged—ready to face the challenges and surprises of life.

God always listens quietly when you share your struggles, problems, dreams, and hopes with Him. But more than that, God has words of encouragement, guidance, and love to share with you in response.

God often speaks in a very soft whisper. Read 1 Kings 19:11–13.

God's Holy Spirit, who lives inside every believer, speaks to your spirit, reminding you of the promises in God's Word. The Holy Spirit also leads you to passages of Scripture that will instruct you in God's ways.

If you are to hear the voice of the Holy Spirit, you will need to spend quiet time with God where there are no distractions. As you have your quiet times of prayer and Bible study, allow a few minutes where you do nothing but *sit and listen* for the voice of God. Allow time for God to give you a tender reply to your thoughts and prayers. Remember, He is the most perfect of all friends and has life-giving advice suited just for you and your unique circumstances—all the days of your life.

When you quiet yourself and tell God that you are ready to listen, you are telling Him that you are interested in what He has to say. As you listen quietly, God may fill your mind with an answer to a problem you are facing. God may nudge you to speak to someone about Jesus. God may show you an area of your life where you are not following Him. He might give you new understanding about a verse in the Bible you just read.

If it is hard for you to sit still, don't worry. Listening to God, just like prayer, takes practice. If you get distracted and your mind wanders, don't get discouraged. Just bring your mind back to your conversation with God. If you don't hear God saying anything specific, that is okay too. Sometimes He just breathes His peace and joy into our hearts, and that speaks more than words.

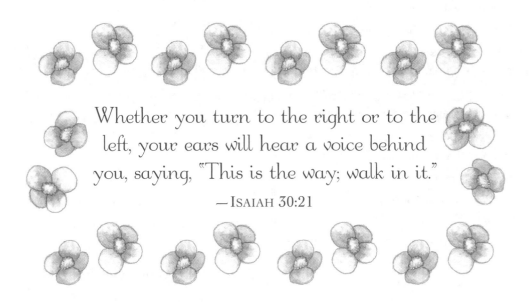

Whether you turn to the right or to the left, your ears will hear a voice behind you, saying, "This is the way; walk in it."

—ISAIAH 30:21

Sometimes when all is quiet, my mind will suddenly be struck with thoughts of praying for certain people. There are different people who will enter my mind, and I say a quick prayer for them. Or occasionally a face I've never seen before will appear, and I offer a prayer to whatever their need or problem may be. I feel that the simplest prayer (even not knowing what you're praying for) has meaning.

Elise E., age 12

Chapter 7
God's Answers to Prayer

God always responds to our prayers. He never ignores us. As we learned in Chapter 1, He is the perfect parent. First John 3:1 says, "How great is the love the Father has lavished on us, that we should be called children of God!" Because of your faith and salvation in Jesus, you *are* a child of God.

The Lord is delighted with you as any loving parent is with his or her child. He longs to give you good things. Matthew 7:11 says that earthly fathers love to give good things to their children; think how much more your perfect, Heavenly Father longs to give good things to His children when they ask.

But sometimes God cannot answer yes to our prayers and give us everything we ask for, because it is not always best for us. And sometimes we have to wait longer than we would like for the answer to come. God is so much wiser and knows things we do not. We may not understand why we can't have something that seems so good and right. But we must trust that God is in control of our lives and is working according to His *perfect* plan.

 Listening for God's Answers

Prayer Skills

There should be no doubt that when we pray, God hears us. The question is, do we hear God when we pray? Do we stop and listen for Him to answer? What would happen if we gave God a chance to talk back? What might happen if, at the end of a prayer, you waited to hear what He had to say in response? After all, we pray so that God will respond with an answer or word of encouragement.

One of the easiest ways to practice "listening prayer" is a prayer journal. To get started, find a quiet place free of distractions. All you need is a pen and a notebook or journal. Begin by writing your prayer, just as you would say it, one sentence or topic at a time. Then listen. Listen to your heart. That is where the Holy Spirit dwells. When you hear Him speak, write down what you hear. At first you may only hear a few words, but as you practice you will begin hearing whole sentences, paragraphs, and possibly pages!

Sometimes it is easiest to train your spiritual ears to hear God's voice if you begin by asking a question, because then you are tuning your ears to hear an answer to that question. Of course, God will speak to you with or without journaling your conversations with Him, but it is a fun exercise that draws you closer to Him and trains your spiritual ears to hear your Shepherd's voice. God has a lot to say to you if only you will listen to Him.

These are some of the benefits of listening prayer:
> You have more confidence in your Christian journey.
> You have more intimacy in your relationship with Jesus Christ.
> You have God's wisdom and insight as it relates to your personal issues.
> You have a personal record of God's words to you as He answers you.

"My thoughts are not your thoughts, neither are your ways my ways," declares the LORD. "As the heavens are higher than the earth, so are my ways higher than your ways and my thoughts than your thoughts. As the rain and the snow come down from heaven, and do not return to it without watering the earth and making it bud and flourish, so that it yields seed for the sower and bread for the eater, so is my word that goes out from my mouth: It will not return to me empty, but will accomplish what I desire and achieve the purpose for which I sent it."

—ISAIAH 55:8–11

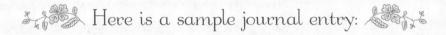 Here is a sample journal entry:

Me: Jesus, this girl at school is trying to win my friendship, but she is so obnoxious that I really don't enjoy being with her at all. What should I do?

Jesus: She is lonely. I love her; can you?

Me: Well, yeah, I can love her, but do I have to spend time with her?

Jesus: Like I said, she is lonely.

Me: Jesus, none of my other friends give this girl any attention. I think she just moved here. I am afraid of losing my other friends or being made fun of.

Jesus: I know just what that feels like. Outcasts and needy people often wanted My attention. My best friends deserted Me when I needed them most. Doing the right thing is not always popular.

Me: Thank You, Jesus, for hearing me, for speaking to me. Give me strength to do the right thing.

Jesus: I am with you always.

> Prayer is very special to me because I know God can always hear me, and He always answers prayer, whether it's right then, a few days later, or even a few months later. He's always there for us in our time of need or when we just want to talk to Him. He always has time for us.
>
> Cherith B., age 10

God can be very creative when He answers our prayers. Imagine what King Hezekiah must have thought when God answered his prayer by sending the angel of the Lord into his enemy's camp, slaying thousands! (See "An Amazing Answer" below.) We must be totally surrendered to God, allowing Him to answer our prayers however He wishes. When we lay down our requests before God, we must also lay down our own expectations of how God should answer.

God loves you! He wants the very best for you! He has promised to hear you when you pray. No request is too small or personal. God even pays attention to requests made by small children for what we would consider insignificant things. Read how God answered the prayers of a little girl in the following story:

An Amazing Answer

God is so faithful. Even back in Bible times, men and women knew they could call upon the name of the Lord and He would help them. In this story taken from Isaiah 37, read how a king called out for God's help during a time of trouble, and see God's amazing answer:

Pictures of Prayer

King Hezekiah held his head in his hands. His country was in a heap of trouble. Already the Assyrian army had captured all the surrounding walled cities in the country of Judah. Only Jerusalem remained free. The Assyrian army had approached once but withdrew to fight another country. Hezekiah knew they would be back.

A shuffle at the door made Hezekiah lift up his head. "What is it, Shebna?" he asked his secretary.

"There are some messengers from the Assyrian king to see you, my Lord." The messengers didn't even manage a bow as they thrust a scroll toward Hezekiah then spun on their heels to leave. Hezekiah slit his nail through the wax and read the letter. He uttered a groan that came from the bottom of his soul.

"My King, what is it?" asked Shebna.

"The Assyrians are threatening to come back. The Assyrian king reminds me that no country has withstood the power of the

Four-year-old Katherine begged her mom for her favorite boxed macaroni-and-cheese dinner. Katherine's mom told her they didn't have any in the cupboard. "Can't we go to the store?" Katherine asked her mom. Katherine's family was very poor at the time, so her mom told her they couldn't buy that particular brand until it was on sale.

Even at four years old, Katherine knew her family always prayed about everything. "Why don't we pray for a sale?" Katherine asked.

"Why don't you pray?" her mom suggested. So Katherine prayed, "Please, God, make macaroni and cheese go on sale."

The next day, Katherine's mom opened the paper looking for the food ads. On the front page of one of the circulars was a sale on Katherine's favorite brand of macaroni and cheese, one of the cheapest prices the family had ever seen.

Assyrian army. He mocks our Holy God, saying our God cannot protect us from the great Assyrians."

"How arrogant!" Shebna exclaimed, but Hezekiah hardly heard him. He strode toward the door, Shebna close behind him. Hezekiah walked straight to the Temple of God, spread the letter from the Assyrians on the floor before the altar, then knelt.

"O Lord Almighty," he prayed. "Listen to the threats the Assyrians have made. They are mocking You, O Lord. Deliver us, God, so that all the kingdoms will know that You are the most powerful, that You alone are God!"

The prophet Isaiah heard about the letter.

He sent a message from the Lord to reassure King Hezekiah of God's care and protection. Soon the people of Jerusalem were confident that God would deliver them.

The angel of the Lord entered the Assyrian camp at night and put to death 185,000 Assyrian soldiers. That's a lot of people! It was so devastating that the king of Assyria moved his army back home to his capital city. Not long afterward, the Assyrian king was assassinated while worshiping his false god. The Lord God had answered Hezekiah's prayer for deliverance!

How has God provided for your family? Is there a prayer God has answered that has encouraged you? Have you ever been surprised at how God has answered your prayers?

All prayer is answered, but the answers may come in different forms. Here are the different responses God may give to your prayers:

[1] yes

[2] no

[3] not now

[4] not this; I've got another plan

[5] be patient, I'm working on the answer even though you can't see it.

If you think God has not answered your prayer, you might actually be missing His answer. Your prayer may have been too general, and that can make it hard to see how God has answered. For example, avoid vague prayers like, "God, bless my mother." It is hard to see how God is answering that prayer. Instead, try praying for her more specifically like, "God, help my mom get that promotion at work." Now this is a prayer where you will see a definite answer! (See Chapter 5 for a refresher on praying specific and direct prayers.)

Sometimes you might be looking for God to do something really big and awesome, when He might be answering in a number of small ways. If someone is sick, perhaps you are praying that this person will get well. God's best might be for that person to accept Christ or lead others to Christ because of her faith demonstrated through the sickness. If you don't see God's answer to your prayer, ask Him about it. Pray, "Lord, show me how You are working in this situation."

How do you know if God is talking to you? That's a good question. Sometimes our minds might be thinking about what *we* want rather than what *God* wants. We must be careful that we don't allow Satan to deceive us. How do you tell the difference?

Check your impression against what the Bible says. God will not tell you something that goes against His Word. God won't tell you to steal something when the Bible says very plainly, "Don't steal." If you don't know what the Bible says about a certain topic, try finding the answer by using a concordance or ask a pastor or a godly friend to show you where you might find the answer in the Bible.

Even so, be careful. Satan can and will misquote Scripture. Satan will try to get you to misunderstand the meaning of God's Word just like he did to Adam and Eve (see Genesis 3:1). Satan will use Scripture to try to get you to do something wrong, like when he tempted Jesus (see Matthew 4:5–7). If you think this could be happening, check to see what else God's Word says on the subject and seek out godly friends to help.

Once you feel God impressing you with a thought and you have checked its truth

Joy Journal

Every time you see how God has answered a prayer, write the story in a notebook. The next time you want to pray for something that you feel is a big request, read through your "joy journal" and see how God has answered your prayers. You'll be encouraged to trust that God can and will answer again.

Testimony Reporter

Ask your friends and family how God has answered prayers for them. Write the stories down like a news reporter would. Using a desktop publishing program, put together your own newsletter comprised of all the stories of how God has answered prayer. Distribute the newsletter to those who have contributed. You will all be heartened to read how God has worked in other people's lives.

Shadow-Box Prayers
by Allison H., age 14

Prayer Projects

My aunt and uncle have a shadow box that hangs on their wall. In the tiny compartments are visual reminders of answered prayer. For example, in one of the compartments is a circus ticket. My cousin had been praying for an opportunity to go to the circus. Then one day, a woman from their church gave my cousin tickets to go to the circus, and she didn't even know that my cousin had been praying for tickets! There are many other small things in the box to help remind their family of answered prayers.

This box also serves as a great opportunity for witnessing. It is quite unusual to see a computer plug or a nail-polish bottle in a shadow box, so naturally people ask about it. This provides a chance for my aunt and uncle to talk to people about all that the Lord has done for them! I think this a great idea to help remind us that the Lord hears our prayers and answers them according to His will.

against His Word (and submitted it to your parents or pastor if it is significant enough), make sure that you act on what God has said. Has God reassured you of His presence with you and His care for you? Keep the conversation going and thank Him for His care. Has He told you to do something kind for someone else? Be sure you do it! Has He pointed out an area of your life where you need to change? Ask for His help, and work at that change.

Never think, however, that God doesn't answer your prayers because you haven't prayed in the right way. God understands what is deep down inside of you. Even when you sometimes can't put those deep feelings into words, He knows what is there and will act to show His mighty power. Remember, the Holy Spirit is your Helper in prayer.

ROMANS 8:26:

> In the same way, the Spirit helps us in our weakness. We do not know what we ought to pray for, but the Spirit himself intercedes for us with groans that words cannot express.

Learning to pray, like most things, is a process. As you grow, you will learn more and more about God and how He answers prayer. You will find your faith beginning to grow for bigger requests, because you have seen His faithfulness in the smaller things. God will do amazing things for those who ask! Don't ever be shy to pray *big* prayers.

If you get discouraged while waiting for God's answers, remember how God has answered your prayers in the past. It will encourage you. You have seen His power and how He is able to provide for you. Let those memories give you faith and courage to ask for His help with the challenges of today and tomorrow.

Action-Packed Prayers

Prayer Ideas

Sometimes you will have prayer requests that are really important to you. You may have difficulty trusting God because the answer doesn't seem to be coming and you're wavering in your faith. In these cases, when the burden seems so heavy, it helps to do something physical to show God that you are choosing to trust and have faith in Him.

In our story about Hezekiah, we saw him intensely upset about the threatening letter from the Assyrians. In desperation, Hezekiah laid out the pages of the letter before the Lord and fell to his knees in deep supplication. We know God knew what was in the letter, but this physical act of taking the letter and laying it down before the Lord helped Hezekiah lay the burden down before God in his heart. He was demonstrating, through a physical action, that He was choosing to trust God to mightily save and deliver.

You can do the same. Set something before the Lord that represents the issue you are struggling with. For example, if you are struggling with a homework assignment, lay the pages and books out before you and lift up a prayer to God, asking for His help and wisdom. Or if you and a close friend have had an argument, take something representative of that person (like a picture of her or an item she has given you) and set it before the Lord. Then pray about the problem and your friendship. If you have many prayer requests, write each request on an index card and then lay all the cards out before you. Begin praying to God, taking each card and praying about the need.

Chapter 8
The Power of Praying with Others

Praying with other people is powerful. When you pray with a group, something wonderful happens—there is unity of heart and mind. Unity among believers greatly pleases God the Father and His Son, Jesus. In fact, Jesus even prayed that His followers would be united: "May they be brought to complete unity to let the world know that you sent me and have loved them even as you have loved me" (John 17:23).

The apostle Paul urged the church to "make every effort to keep the unity of the Spirit through the bond of peace" (Ephesians 4:3). There is a special touch of God's presence when His children come together in prayer. You will feel closer to God and closer to the people in your group when you pray together.

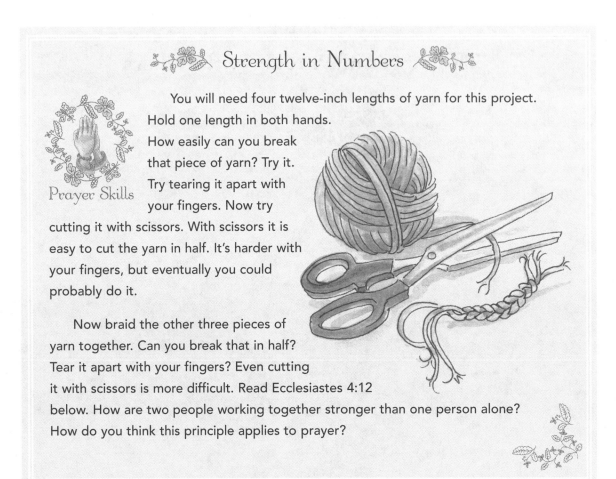

Strength in Numbers

Prayer Skills

You will need four twelve-inch lengths of yarn for this project. Hold one length in both hands. How easily can you break that piece of yarn? Try it. Try tearing it apart with your fingers. Now try cutting it with scissors. With scissors it is easy to cut the yarn in half. It's harder with your fingers, but eventually you could probably do it.

Now braid the other three pieces of yarn together. Can you break that in half? Tear it apart with your fingers? Even cutting it with scissors is more difficult. Read Ecclesiastes 4:12 below. How are two people working together stronger than one person alone? How do you think this principle applies to prayer?

Imagine that you have to color a twelve-foot banner for a school activity. If you take twenty hours to finish the banner by yourself, how long would it take if you had a friend working with you and you both agreed on how it should be done? How long would it take three people to complete the banner?

When people work together, the work gets done faster and people do not get tired from doing the job. This also applies to prayer. People can pray better and more effectively when they pray together. Because God's people are working together to know God's will, God will answer their prayer in mighty ways, so the whole group will be blessed.

> Though one may be overpowered, two can defend themselves. A cord of three strands is not quickly broken. — ECCLESIASTES 4:12

Here are some reasons why group prayer is important:

You get the full counsel (fuller understanding) of God together and can then pray more effectively about what God is wanting to do.

You become closer to the people you pray with because you share the same faith with them.

You see God answering other people's prayers besides your own, and that is an encouragement in your personal walk of faith.

Faith is contagious. Each person brings her flame of faith. Together you have a roaring fire! This will accomplish much!

It is encouraging to hear others pray for the things that you are also concerned about.

You can learn how to pray by listening to others pray.

An army can do a lot more damage to the enemy than a single soldier!

Uniting in prayer with believers gives you more confidence to draw near to God. God knows the need even before you ask. But how pleased He is to see His people unite in agreement, bringing all prayer needs to Him!

E-mail Prayer Newsletter

Prayer Ideas

If you love e-mail, set up a prayer newsletter group with a few close friends. Every week, each person can post her prayer requests. Write out your prayers for one another and send them in an e-mail. You will all be mutually encouraged, knowing you are actively praying for one another.

Agreeing in Prayer

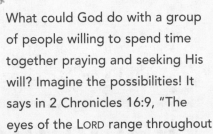

Pictures of Prayer

What could God do with a group of people willing to spend time together praying and seeking His will? Imagine the possibilities! It says in 2 Chronicles 16:9, "The eyes of the LORD range throughout the earth to strengthen those whose hearts are fully committed to him." In the following story taken from Acts 12:1–17, read what happened when a group of people gathered in prayer to seek God's help for a friend:

It was a quiet, sad group of believers that snuck under the cover of darkness into Mary's home. It was one of the darkest hours the new church had faced. The believers were still in shock that James, one of Jesus' disciples, was dead. Now Peter was in prison and destined for the same fate.

In spite of the tragedy of James' death, the group of believers still held on to their faith, believing that God had the power to work on Peter's behalf. Yet they weren't quite prepared for how God would answer their prayers. Fervently they prayed, finding comfort and encouragement in being together. They were so focused on their prayers, they hardly noticed when Rhoda, the servant girl, slipped out of the room to answer a knock at the gate.

A squeal cut short their prayers. "Peter," Rhoda gasped, "Peter's at the gate!"

"You're out of your mind, girl," one believer said, forgetting what they had gathered to pray about. *Poor Rhoda!* thought the believer.

Internet Prayer Chain
by Abby S., age 13

Prayer Ideas

A great way to communicate who needs prayers is by the Internet! List the people that need prayers and why they need them. Then send the list to your friends, requesting them to add to your existing list the people they know of who need prayer and then send the list to their friends. Soon, a prayer chain will be going. Don't forget to pray for those people that your friends requested. You could even set aside a certain time during the day to pray particularly for the people your friends requested. God will do powerful things with prayer!

Grief does funny things to people. And it is dark outside. She wants so badly for Peter to be alive. She must have assumed the person at the gate was Peter.

"No, no, it *is* Peter," Rhoda insisted. A persistent knocking punctuated her words.

"Maybe it's his angel," another believer offered, thinking, *Surely God has sent an angel to comfort us in our grief.*

The knocking continued. Mary and the others went to the door. There stood Peter, very much alive. Cries of astonishment and delight filled the doorway, but Peter waved with his hand to quiet them. He gently closed the gate.

"How did you get out of prison?" one believer finally asked.

"God's angel delivered me," Peter answered. "I was asleep, chained between two guards. The angel woke me and told me to put on my coat and follow him. I thought I was dreaming until the angel led me outside to the street. The cold night air assured me I was awake!"

The group murmured amazement and praise to God, but again, Peter held up his hand. "I'm not safe even here. Tell Jesus' brothers and the other apostles what has happened," and he slipped out the door into the night.

God's people had met together to pray, and God had answered in a mighty way!

Prayer Circle
by Kristin P.

Prayer Projects

It's great to get together with friends to pray, but at first, some friends might feel uncomfortable praying out loud together. It takes time to build trust in each other and for everyone to feel comfortable. Here's a way to make praying together easier.

Invite some friends over to your house. Get everyone to sit in a circle. Give each friend two sheets of paper and a pencil, and ask each person to put her name at the top of each paper. Give your friends these directions: On one sheet of paper, write down something you personally need prayer for. On the other sheet of paper, write a person's name that you know needs prayer.

Pass your two sheets of paper to the person on your right. Take turns praying for the prayer needs listed on the paper. You can continue to pass them around two or more times, completing the circle.

Prayer is an important thing in life. God wants us to talk with Him. Sometimes it may be boring, but the Spirit of God can move in ways we can't even comprehend. I suggest praying with a close Christian friend. It's awesome to see how God moves in so many different ways.

Shereen W., age 11

For where two or three come together in my name, there am I with them. — MATTHEW 18:20

Prayer Partners
by Shayna J., age 15

Prayer Projects

A fun and effective way to remember to pray, and a good way to have fun, is to have a prayer partner. That's what we do at my church. The first thing you do is pick one or two people to choose the partners. We picked our pastor and our choir leader. Every day for one month, they pray and ask God to help them see who should be partnered together.

After announcing the partners, the two people who are partnered together get a piece of paper and write down everyone and everything they need prayer for. The list is then put into an envelope for one of the partners to keep. This helps keep the needs confidential. The partners pray every day for each other and their list of requests.

The partners are responsible for each other, and when one partner misses church, the other is to call to check on the absent one. That way, when someone needs prayer, the person can just call on his or her partner. This is a great way to get to know each other a little better. We learn so much about each other. You can do anything with this idea. At my church, we switch partners every five months. You get to spend time with people you never really knew. It is so fun!

G.A.P.P.—Girls Appointed Prayer Partners
by Carolyn C., age 13

Prayer Ideas

Something my youth group started awhile back was a group for girls. Our youth pastor gave us free control to turn the group into whatever we felt we needed the most to grow in our faith. At first we weren't sure how we wanted to run the group. We all had different needs (the people in our youth group come from all different types of backgrounds) and we all wanted them fulfilled. Then one of the girls suggested that we turn the group into a prayer group. That way we could all help one another and also be helped in return. We gave ourselves the name G.A.P.P.—Girls Appointed Prayer Partners.

We meet one Sunday every month. At first we just talk about what God has been doing in our lives. Then we break off into our small groups (usually no more than two or three) and privately tell each other our prayer needs. At the end of the hour, we break off individually and just talk to God about, well ... anything! This is really a great way to help each other grow in faith and also to know that there is someone who is praying for you!

Praying as a Group

Group prayer is a wonderful experience. But, just like personal prayer and listening to God, it takes practice. Here are some ideas to get your group sold on praying together. For more creative ideas, see the prayer projects throughout this chapter and book.

Give one-sentence praise reports

Give one-sentence praise reports. Have your group form a circle. Ask each person to speak one sentence, thanking God for something. This is easier to do for girls who are shy about praying out loud.

circle prayer

When you have a circle prayer, have each person pray for only one need. That way, the prayer time will go more quickly.

share a need or praise

When a person shares a need or praise, stop and pray right away for that need only. Then move on to the next person.

Conversational prayer. Before praying together, make a list of the things you want to pray about. Choose a leader. The leader will read aloud the first prayer need on the list. People in the group take turns praying for only that one topic. You don't have to go in a circle and not everyone has to pray. Each person should pray only if she wants to. You can learn to pray for different things about that topic. For example, if the father of a person in the group lost his job, people might pray for the following:

God would help him find a job.

God would provide for the family's needs until he finds a job.

God would help the family trust Him rather than worry.

God would show the group how they can help.

When the group has been quiet for a few seconds, the group leader can announce the next topic of prayer. Continue to pray conversationally until you have reached the end of the list, then the leader can say a final prayer.

You and your group will be blessed beyond measure as you share one another's burdens together in prayer. There are really no words to describe the joy and supernatural intensity that comes from praying in agreement with other believers—you'll just have to experience it for yourself!

Prayer Bulletin Board
by Megan M., age 11

Prayer Projects

A prayer board is a good place to share prayer requests. You will need: two or three pieces of cardboard, glue, pins, blank index cards, a pencil, and some string. Glue the cardboard pieces together, then put the board up somewhere in the house, so your family can put prayer requests on it. Attach the pencil to the string, then attach the other end of the string to the board. Tack the blank index cards onto the board, so they are available when needed. Make sure you restock the board with new index cards and take down prayer requests when they've been answered.

Friendship Diary
by Esther B.

Prayer Projects

Agree with your friend and prayer partner to keep a diary of prayer needs and answers for one week. Then exchange diaries. Write in your friend's diary. Read her entries and pray for her, her needs, and her faith walk. Pray that she grows to be more like Jesus. Keep exchanging diaries. After a year, each of you can see how much you've grown in the Lord and how God has answered your prayers. If you do this with a friend who lives out of town, you might want to exchange diaries every month instead of each week.

Prayer is really special to me. It means time alone to just talk to God, and to share my thoughts, problems, and joy with Him. I know that God knows everything that I want to tell Him before I do, but I still feel better when I take it to Him in prayer. After I share my problems or sadness with God, I feel a burden lifted in my spirit and a special peace. I know that is the peace of Jesus Christ.

—Gabrielle E., age 11

Prayer Board Game
by Greta D.

Prayer Projects

This is a way to make prayer fun! Take an old board game (Sorry, Parcheesi, Candyland, or any-thing), and write down the names of all the people you can think of on the board spaces. Play the game as usual, and when you land on a space, you pray for the person whose name is on that space! It makes prayer fun! I think it's important to pray for everything because it brings you closer to God. But a lot of people think that it's boring to pray, so I'm making it fun!

Spare-Time Prayer
by Karen S., age 15

Prayer Ideas

I find that I often have time left at the end of my exams (even after checking my answers). This is a great time to pray because everything around me is quiet, and I am able to concen-trate. Talking to God also calms me down. While on the subject of exams, I tend to pray before them as well.

Prayer Basket

Prayer Projects

This is a good activity to do with your family. Put a small bowl or basket in a prominent place in your house (like the dining-room table or kitchen counter). Fill it with a pen and small blank slips of paper or index cards cut in half. Throughout the day, family members can write prayer requests and praise notes on the papers, fold them, and place them back in the basket. No peeking at prayer requests till prayer time!

At the end of the day, have a family prayer circle. Let each person take a paper out of the basket until the papers are all gone. Leave the blank papers for the next day. As your family takes turns praying, each family member can either thank God for the praise report or pray for the petition that is on the paper he or she has drawn.

Praise/Prayer Jar
by T. K. R.

Prayer Projects

A praise/prayer jar can hold praise reports and prayer needs so that as friends and family think of prayers, they can write them down immediately. Then, when you get together, you can read and pray for the requests together.

Supplies: a mayonnaise or apple-sauce jar, tissue paper, glue, water, and strips of tissue paper. Mix equal parts of glue and water in a shallow bowl or aluminum pie pan. Dip the small pieces of tissue paper into the glue mixture. Decoratively wrap the tissue paper around your jar. Allow it to dry overnight.

LORD, I have heard of your fame; I stand in awe of your deeds, O LORD. Renew them in our day, in our time make them known; in wrath remember mercy.

(A prayer from Habakkuk 3:2)

☆ ☆ ☆ See You at the Pole ☆ ☆ ☆

Prayer Ideas

Plan a prayer gathering for your school where students gather around the school flagpole to pray for the school, the teachers, the students, and their families. You can coordinate this with the official annual *See You at the Pole* event, but you can also have your own *See You at the Pole* events anytime of the year.

You can even plan a prayer party around the time of the annual event. For your party, you can prepare a dessert, such as the following:

☆ AMERICAN PRAYER CUPCAKES ☆

☆ Supplies: 1 cake mix, 1 can prepared icing, red, white, and blue sprinkles, toothpicks, small slips of paper, transparent tape, red and blue fine-tipped markers

☆ Directions: Make cupcakes according to the directions on the cake-mix box, with an adult's supervision. When the cupcakes cool, apply the icing and sprinkles.

While the cupcakes are baking, prepare the party favors for the tops of the cupcakes. Draw a red line along the top edge of each slip of paper, then a blue line along the bottom edge. Fold the paper in half. In the middle, on one side, write the name of a national leader, local leader, church leader, or schoolteacher. Tape your "flag" to the top of a toothpick. After you have iced the cupcakes, insert a flag into each cupcake. At your party, after you have enjoyed dessert, sit in a circle. Ask each person to pray for the person mentioned on his or her cupcake flag. Here are some things you can pray for:

☆ Thank God for the leader.

☆ Ask God to give the leader extra energy.

☆ Ask God to give the person wisdom in making decisions.

☆ Ask God to give the leader courage to do what is right, to do what God would want, not necessarily what would make him or her popular.

Chapter 9
Encouraging People through Prayer

Words and prayers of encouragement are so vital for our life of faith. Proverbs 18:21 says, "The tongue has the power of life and death." When we speak words of encouragement to one another, we speak words that bring life; words that nourish and strengthen our spirits, enabling us to "run with perseverance the race marked out for us" (Hebrews 12:1).

When we encourage others with our words and prayers, we hearten them—inspire, cheer, reassure, comfort, fortify, and embolden them.

Encourage one another and build each other up, just as in fact you are doing.

—1 THESSALONIANS 5:11

Encouraging Words

Prayer Skills

Writing a thank-you note to someone who has told you that she has been praying for you is a very kind thing to do. Tell the person how it made you feel to know this.

If God lays someone on *your* heart, write that person a note, letting the individual know that you are praying for her. This will be an encouragement to your friend, just as others' prayers are an encouragement to you.

Your love has given me great joy and encouragement, because you, brother, have refreshed the hearts of the saints. —PHILEMON 7

It is important to pray for others. It's also important to let others know you are praying for them and how you have *specifically* prayed for them. When you pray for people, you bring their needs before God. You show God that you care about other people as much, if not more, than you care about yourself and your own needs.

The following true story illustrates this point. When a three-week-old baby needed eye surgery, people from churches in six different states prayed for that baby and her family. The dad was out of work, the family had no insurance, and the medical bills amounted to ten thousand dollars. The baby came through the surgeries fine, and God helped the family pay the medical bills in a marvelous way.

How do you think the prayers of so many people were an encouragement to this family?

Telling a friend that you are praying for her will encourage her because she will have a chance to see God at work. You become a reflection of God's love, and she is reminded of God's care for her. Your prayers demonstrate God's faithfulness to your friends.

> Let us not become weary in doing good, for at the proper time we will reap a harvest if we do not give up. Therefore, as we have opportunity, let us do good to all people, especially to those who belong to the family of believers. —GALATIANS 6:9–10

Praying "on the Spot"

Have you ever said to someone, "Will you pray for me?" and that person said, "Yes, let me pray for you right now"? This might have taken you off guard. You may have felt a bit uncomfortable at first. But when someone prays for you right on the spot, it can feel like a warm blanket of love being wrapped around you. It is very encouraging when someone verbally prays for you in your presence.

You can do the same for other people, although this takes a lot of boldness. It's easy to say, "I'll pray for you," when someone shares a struggle. But it means a lot more when you actually stop and take a moment to pray out loud for the person, right then and

---

E-mail Prayer Letter
by Karen S.

Prayer Ideas

By praying for others, you can encourage them to pass on the blessing of praying for others too. Select a friend you would like to pray for. Send an e-mail to your friend similar to the one below. Encourage your friend to pass on the blessing of praying for others by e-mailing someone else and praying for that person.

Dear _____,

I just wanted to tell you that I am praying for you today. I thank God for the person He has made you to be. I love you and I know God loves you too.

I'd like this to be a prayer-chain e-mail. If you would like to be a part of it here's what I suggest. First, pray for me today. Next, pass on the blessing of prayer by sending this letter to another person you know. **Don't** hit your Forward button. Instead, copy and paste this letter 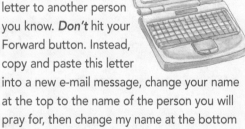 into a new e-mail message, change your name at the top to the name of the person you will pray for, then change my name at the bottom to your name.

You don't have to send this back to me. Just remember to pray for me and for your special prayer friend. And remember that I'm praying for you too!

Your friend, _____

there. The individual will know you sincerely care and can immediately receive encouragement and ministry from your prayer.

More Ways to Show You Care

It's one thing to tell people you are praying for them. Your words will mean much more when you *show* them that you are praying and that you are also willing to get involved in their lives. You demonstrate your faith in God when you are willing to be a part of God's answer to meet others' needs.

Think about the people who are currently on your prayer list. How can you encourage them? How can you help them? Don't know? Ask God to show you how you can be a blessing in these people's lives! The prayer projects in this chapter can give you ideas to get you going.

Read the following three Scriptures from the book of Acts to see how the apostle Paul's friends encouraged him. Discover new ways of showing your friends that you are supporting them.

Jesus' Time of Need

Pictures of Prayer

Remember when, as written in Matthew 26, Jesus went to the Garden of Gethsemane with His disciples to pray? He was very troubled. He needed their support and prayers. As Jesus pulled three disciples aside, He expressed His deep sorrow and despair to them: *"My soul is overwhelmed with sorrow to the point of death. Stay here and keep watch with me"* (v. 38).

With great emotion, Jesus fell to the ground and prayed: *"My Father, if it is possible, may this cup be taken from me. Yet not as I will, but as you will"* (v. 39). Jesus knew that the next day He would die for the sins of the world. The human side of Him didn't want to go through the terrible suffering. Yet as the Son of God, He was willing to follow through with God's great plan for mankind.

When he had said this, he knelt down with all of them and prayed. They all wept as they embraced him and kissed him. —Acts 20:36–37

When our time was up, we left and continued on our way. All the disciples and their wives and children accompanied us out of the city, and there on the beach we knelt to pray. —Acts 21:5

There we found some brothers who invited us to spend a week with them. And so we came to Rome. The brothers there had heard that we were coming, and they traveled as far as the Forum of Appius and the Three Taverns to meet us. At the sight of these men Paul thanked God and was encouraged.
—Acts 28:14–15

Cookie Prayers

Prayer Ideas

Make a batch of home-made cookies for an elderly friend, a teacher, a school secretary, or a church leader. As you make the cookies, pray for that person. When you give the cookies to your friend, include a note, telling the person you have been praying for him or her.

When Jesus came back from an intense time of prayer, He found the disciples asleep. *"Could you men not keep watch with me for one hour?… Watch and pray so that you will not fall into temptation. The spirit is willing, but the body is weak"* (vv. 40–41). Through sleepy eyes, the disciples watched Him go back to pray. Then once again, they promptly fell asleep.

In Jesus' darkest hour, He needed support and encouragement from His disciples, just like we need it from our friends and family, and just like our friends and family need it from us. It's important to be sensitive to the prayer needs of those around us and not grow "tired" like Jesus' disciples did in the Garden of Gethsemane. Our prayers matter, and they really do encourage those who ask for our prayers.

These believers took time to be with Paul. Some even traveled with their children so that they could pray with him. Simple acts of kindness, like seeing someone off on a journey, can be a real encouragement. Sharing tears, laughter, hurts, and sorrows with fellow believers is one of the greatest privileges and greatest joys we can experience on this earth. Don't shy away from embracing people and sharing in their triumphs and defeats. God brings these special moments into our lives so that the body of Christ can be united as one.

How beautiful on the mountains are the feet of those who bring good news, who proclaim peace, who bring good tidings, who proclaim salvation, who say to Zion, "Your God reigns!"

—ISAIAH 52:7

Prayer Scrolls

Prayer Projects

It's important to tell others you are praying for them. When life gets hard, they'll be encouraged to stay faithful to Jesus as they remember someone is praying for them. Here is a creative way to tell a friend you are praying for her.

Supplies:

Small sheets of colored paper, tissue paper, ribbon, and a plastic sandwich bag (optional).

Directions:

Write a message to your friend or family member on a slip of paper, telling her you are praying for her. You can also include a favorite Bible verse. Roll up the paper like a scroll. Then wrap tissue paper around the scroll and secure it with a ribbon and pretty bow. Put the prayer scroll where she will find it. You can leave it on her pillow, or you can slip it into a sandwich bag and tape the bag on her bathroom mirror or bedroom door.

Secret Prayer Partners

Prayer Ideas

Choose a missionary, teacher, or church leader whom you would like to pray for on a regular basis. Send a note to that person to explain what you want to do. Ask if there is anything specific you can pray about. If you feel nervous about revealing who you are, you can still send a note saying that you are praying and sign the note, "Your special prayer partner." One advantage, however, to telling the person who you are is that the individual can share specific needs with you. Don't forget to pray for your person every day!

Prayers 'n' Brownies

Prayer Ideas

Share these brownies with a friend who needs some encouragement and could use some reassurance from your prayers. This is also a great recipe to make for a teacher, church leader, or other adult leader who needs encouragement. Have an adult assist you with the microwave and oven. Write a note to go with the brownies that tells the person that you are praying.

Best Ever Brownies:
Ingredients:
2 cups sugar
4 eggs
2 sticks margarine or butter
2 cups flour
1 cup cocoa
2 teaspoons vanilla
1 cup chopped nuts

Directions:
Beat the sugar and eggs together.
Melt the margarine in a glass bowl in the microwave for 1 minute.
Add to sugar mixture and beat well.
Add flour, cocoa, vanilla, and nuts; stir until well mixed.
Spread in a lightly greased 10-x-15-inch jelly-roll pan (a cookie sheet with sides).
Bake in a 325-degree oven for 20 minutes.
Remove from oven; cool for 10 minutes.
Cut into squares and place on a separate plate.

Prayer Ideas

Prayer Picnic

Everyone loves to go on a picnic on a beautiful day. You can invite your friends for a prayer picnic, and they will certainly go home blessed and encouraged.

Have your picnic in a backyard or a park. If rain threatens to spoil your plans, spread a blanket on the floor of your family room and have your picnic indoors. Send invitations for the prayer picnic one week in advance. Ask each friend to bring a picnic basket of her favorite picnic lunch to share. You can then share lunches with each other. You could offer to provide drinks.

Here are some ideas for activities you can do at the prayer picnic:

Popcorn Prayer Activity

These are short prayers, one-sentence prayers that you can pray as needs come to mind. Teach your friends about popcorn prayers this way: Before your picnic, fix a bag of microwave popcorn. Place it in the middle of your picnic blanket. You can pray popcorn prayers one of two ways:

Throughout your picnic, as your friends think of prayers, they can take a piece of popcorn from the bag, pray their sentence prayer out loud, then eat the piece of popcorn. No popcorn eating without praying first!

End your picnic by praying sentence/popcorn prayers. Sit in a circle. Each person can take a piece of popcorn, say a sentence prayer about anything (thanking God or a request), then eat the piece of popcorn.

Alphabet Thanks

After you eat your picnic food, sit in a circle. The first person must think of something she is thankful for that begins with the letter *A*. The next person says something she is thankful for that starts with the letter *B*. Go around the circle until you have gone through the alphabet.

Make this game more challenging. Have each person name all the things for which thanks has already been mentioned before moving on to the next letter.

Basket of Blessings

Place a basket in the middle of your picnic blanket. As guests arrive, give them several index cards and a pencil. Ask them to write a blessing or something they are thankful for on the card. They must sign their name on the card. When you have finished your picnic lunch, ask one person at a time to draw a card out of the basket and thank God for that blessing. If it is personal to the person who wrote it down, the person praying can thank God for the blessing in the other person's life. For example, "Thank You, God, that Chelsea enjoys her new puppy so much," or "Thank You, God, for Jennifer's family."

Prayer-Partner Promise

Write each person's name on a slip of paper. Fold the papers and put them in a basket. Before your friends leave, have half of the girls select a paper. If anyone draws their own name, have them select another paper. If the last person selects her own name, have everyone put the papers back in the basket and try again. Then have each person who drew a name find her prayer partner. Have each set of prayer partners share prayer needs and pray together before they leave. Promise to be each other's prayer partners for the next week. Plan another picnic or party to find out how God has answered your prayers.

Appendix A— Prayers in the Bible

Deeper Study

Abraham's servant prays for success in his task.

—GENESIS 24:12–14

Isaac prays for his wife to have a baby.

—GENESIS 25:21–22

Jacob prays for his meeting with Esau.

—GENESIS 32:9–12

Miriam sings a song of praise.   —EXODUS 15:1–21

Moses prays for mercy.   —EXODUS 32:11–14

Samson's father prays for wisdom in raising his son.

—JUDGES 13:8

Samson prays for a return of his strength.

—JUDGES 16:28

Hannah prays for a baby.   —1 SAMUEL 1:1–20

Hannah prays a prayer of thanksgiving. —1 SAMUEL 2:1–10

Samuel commits to pray for Israel.   —1 SAMUEL 12:23

Jabez prays for blessing.   —1 CHRONICLES 4:9–10

David prays a prayer of thanksgiving.

—1 CHRONICLES 17:16–27

Solomon prays a prayer to dedicate the temple.

—2 CHRONICLES 6:12–42

Hezekiah prays for deliverance.

—2 CHRONICLES 32:20–21; ISAIAH 37:14–20

Manasseh prays a prayer of repentance.

—2 CHRONICLES 33:10–13, 18–20

Ezra prays a prayer of repentance.   —EZRA 9:5–15

Nehemiah prays for restoration.   —NEHEMIAH 1:4–11

Nehemiah prays, praising God for His works.

—NEHEMIAH 9:5–38

Esther commits to pray and fast before a big decision.

—ESTHER 4:15–17

Job prays for his friends.   —JOB 42:8–10

David prays a prayer of repentance.   —PSALM 51

Daniel prays for God to forgive his country.

—DANIEL 9:4–19

Jonah prays a prayer of thanksgiving and rededication.

—JONAH 2:1–9

Habakkuk prays, praising God's character.

—HABAKKUK 3:1–19

Jesus prays the model prayer.   —MATTHEW 6:9–13

Jesus prays for the children.   —MATTHEW 19:13–15

Jesus prays for deliverance from the Cross.

—MATTHEW 26:36–46

Jesus prays for His new disciples.   —LUKE 6:12

Jesus prays for unity among His disciples.   —JOHN 17

The new church prays together. —ACTS 1:12–14, 2:42–47

The early church prays for courage.   —ACTS 4:24–31

Paul and Barnabas pray for new church leaders, committing them to God.   —ACTS 14:23

The believers at Tyre pray for Paul.   —ACTS 21:5–6

Paul prays for the spiritual growth of the Ephesian church.

—EPHESIANS 1:15–23

Paul prays for the believers' spiritual growth.

—EPHESIANS 3:14–21

Paul prays for the Philippian church. —PHILIPPIANS 1:3–11

Paul prays for the Colossian church. —COLOSSIANS 1:3–14

Epaphras wrestles in prayer for the Colossian church.

—COLOSSIANS 4:12

Appendix B—
Special Promises to Pray

Numbers 23:19 — **God's faithfulness** [God keeps His promises; He does not lie.]

Deuteronomy 31:8 — **God's presence** [God is with you and will not forsake you.]

Joshua 1:9 — **the Lord is with you** [God is with you.]

Psalm 25:14 — **God's trust** [God confides in you and makes His covenant known to you.]

Psalm 37:4 — **heart's desires** [God will give you the desires of your heart.]

Psalm 37:23–25 — **firm steps** [God makes your steps firm; He upholds you.]

Psalm 55:22 — **casting your cares on God** [God will sustain you; He will not let you fall.]

Psalm 73:26 — **God's strength** [God is the strength of your heart, your portion forever.]

Psalm 91 — **God's protection** [God protects you.]

Psalm 100:5 — **God's faithfulness to the generations** [God is good; His love endures forever; He is faithful.]

Psalm 118:5–6 — **God's help** [God sets you free; He is with you.]

Psalm 119:9, 11 — **help in temptation** [Living according to God's Word keeps you from sin.]

Psalm 138:8 — **God's involvement** [God fulfills His purpose for you; His love endures forever; He will not abandon the work of His hands.]

Proverbs 3:3–4 — **favor with God and man** [God gives you favor with Himself and man.]

Proverbs 3:5–6 — **guidance** [God will make your paths straight.]

Isaiah 26:3 — **peace** [God will keep you in perfect peace.]

Isaiah 30:21 — **hearing God** [You will hear God's voice and He will guide you.]

Isaiah 40:31 — **renewed strength** [God will renew your strength.]

Isaiah 41:10 — **God's help** [God is with you; He will strengthen, help, and uphold you.]

Isaiah 43:1–2 — **God's protection** [God has redeemed you and called you by name.]

Jeremiah 29:11–13 — **hope and a future** [God has a plan for you.]

Lamentations 3:22–23 — **God's faithfulness, love, and compassion** [God will be kind to you.]

Matthew 7:7–8 — **God's responsiveness** [God responds to you.]

Matthew 11:28–30 — **rest for your soul** [Jesus gives rest to your soul. He is gentle and humble.]

Matthew 18:20 — **God's presence** [Jesus is with you and other believers.]

John 5:24 — **assurance of salvation** [God gives you assurance of salvation.]

John 15:7 — **answered prayers** [God grants your requests.]

Romans 8:28 — **God works good in your life** [God works for your good in all things.]

Romans 12:2 — **knowing God's will** [God's will is good, pleasing, and perfect.]

2 Corinthians 5:17 — **a new creation** [God makes you a new creature in Christ.]

2 Corinthians 12:9–10 — **strength in weakness** [God makes you strong when you're weak.]

Ephesians 2:10 — **created for a purpose** [God created you for a purpose.]

Philippians 4:6–7 — **peace when anxious** [God's peace will guard your heart and mind.]

Philippians 4:13 — **strength in Christ** [God gives you Christ's strength.]

Philippians 4:19 — **God's provision** [God will meet all your needs.]

2 Timothy 1:7 — **overcoming timidity** [God gives you a spirit of power, love, and sound mind.]

2 Timothy 3:16 — **God's Word being useful** [All of Scripture is God-breathed and useful.]

James 1:12 — **reward for perseverance** [God promises a crown of life to you.]

1 Peter 5:7 — **God's care** [God cares for you.]

1 John 1:9 — **forgiveness of sins** [God forgives your sins and purifies you.]

1 John 5:13 — **assurance of salvation** [God gives you assurance of salvation.]

1 John 5:14–15 — **knowing God's will** [God will grant your requests if you ask according to His will.]

Deeper Study

Appendix C— Psalms to Pray

Some of the psalms are praise songs directed to God. Other psalms are prayers that make requests of God. Many of the prayer psalms end by praising God and showing confidence in His power to overcome the difficulty the writer of the psalm is facing. Yet other psalms talk about God or tell others to praise God. There are psalms that praise God, make requests, and talk about God all in the same psalm!

You can make many of these psalms your personal prayers to God. You can use the praise psalms to praise God and the prayer psalms to pour out your heart to Him. You can even make the teaching personal by changing the word *God* to *You*, then reading the psalm to God. The following is a list of Psalms to get you started.

Psalms of Praise to God:	Psalms Requesting Help from God:	Teaching Psalms:
Psalm 8	Psalm 5	Psalm 19 — God's protection
Psalm 16	Psalm 25	Psalm 23 — Trusting God
Psalm 18	Psalm 31	Psalm 24 — Purity of heart
Psalm 47	Psalm 51	Psalm 27 — God's deliverance
Psalm 48	Psalm 54	Psalm 37 — Godly wisdom
Psalm 65	Psalm 55	Psalm 103 — God's compassion
Psalm 89	Psalm 61	Psalm 106 — Plea for mercy
Psalm 96	Psalm 70	Psalm 107 — God's love
Psalm 100	Psalm 71	Psalm 118 — Thanksgiving
Psalm 113	Psalm 85	Psalm 119 — Devotion to the Word
Psalm 117	Psalm 91	Psalm 121 — God's help
Psalm 134	Psalm 130	
Psalm 135	Psalm 139	
Psalm 136	Psalm 141	
Psalm 145		
Psalm 146		
Psalm 147		
Psalm 148		
Psalm 149		
Psalm 150		

Deeper Study

Appendix D—
The Nature and Character of God from A to Z

God is...

A Almighty, All-Knowing, All-Sufficient, Awesome, Ageless, Abounding in Love, Available, Accessible, Always There, Always Watching, Abba Father, the Alpha, Advisor, Atoning Sacrifice, All-in-All, the Author of Our Faith

B Bold, Brilliant, Beautiful, Bountiful, Benevolent, Our Banner, Burden-Bearer, the Bread of Life

C Caring, Compassionate, Consistent, Constant, Our Crucified Christ, Confronter of Evil, Convicter of Sin, Commander-in-Chief, Counselor, Comforter, Companion, Creative Creator, Our Confidence

D Delightful, Dedicated, Devoted, Dear, Dramatic, Dependable, Daring, Our Destiny-Maker, Deliverer, Defender, Discipler, Discipliner

E Exalted, Excellent, Exceptional, Eternal, Ever-Present, Empathetic, Encourager, Emmanuel (God with Us), El Shaddai (God Almighty), El Roi (the One Who Sees), El Olam (Eternal God), Elohim (God), El Elyon (God Most High), Everlasting Father

F Forgiver, Fair, Free, Faultless, Faithful, Fortress, Friend, Father, Father of Compassion, Finisher of Our Faith

G Gracious, Good, Generous, Giving, Great, Glorious, Gift, Guide, the God of Abraham, Isaac, and Jacob, God of the Covenant, God of All Comfort, the God of Israel, Our Glory

H Holy, Honest, High and Lifted Up, Our Hope, Helper, Healer, Husband, Hiding Place, Heavenly Father, the Holy Spirit, the Holy One of Israel

I Integrity, Infinite, Indwelling, Insightful, Inspiring, Innermost, Impartial, Invaluable, I AM WHO I AM, Immanuel (God with Us)

J Just, Judge, Joy, Jealous, Justifier, Jesus, Jehovah, Jehovah Jireh (Our Provider), Jehovah Nissi (Our Banner), Jehovah Tsidkenu (Our Righteousness), Jehovah Shalom (Our Peace), Jehovah Shammah (He Who Is There), Jehovah Rophe (Our Healer), Jehovah M'Kaddesh (Our Sanctifier), Jehovah Rohi (Our Shepherd)

K Kind, Knowledge, King, King of Kings, King of Hosts, King of the Jews, Our Keeper

L Lord, Lord of Lords, Living God, Living Word, Living Water, Lamb of God, Light, Lovely, Longsuffering, Loyal, Leader, Love, Loving, the Life

M Mighty, Majestic, Merciful, Molder, Master, Maker, Most High God, Messiah, Matchless

N Near, Never-Ending, the Name Above All Names

O Omnipotent, Omnipresent, Omniscient, Only God, Omega, the One True God, Our Overseer, Our Owner

P Pure, Powerful, Present, Perfect, Personal, Persistent, Precious, Patient, Our Peace, Potter, Provider, Protector, the Prince of Peace, the One Who Pardons Us

Q Quiet, Quick to Love, Quick to Listen, Quotable, Qualified

R Righteous, Real, Royalty, Risen, Responsive, Rich in Love, Refreshing, Reliable, Radiant, Rock, Restorer, Redeemer, Rescuer, Ruler of All, Our Refiner, Our Reward

S Savior, Sought-After, Supreme, Spirit, Special, Sincere, Sinless, Strong, Our Strength, Sovereign, Steadfast, Slow to Anger, Sacrifice, Stronghold, Shield, Strong Tower, Security, Shepherd, Sanctifier, Salvation, the Son of God, the Son of David, the Son of Man, Our Sustainer, Our Shelter

T True, Timely, Triumphant, Tremendous, Tender, Teacher, the Trinity, the Truth, Tender, Trustworthy, Our Treasure, Transformer

U Undefeated, Unequaled, Uncompromising, Unlimited, Unceasing, Ultimate, Undaunted, Unchanging, Understanding, Unfailing, Unconditional Love

V Valiant, Victorious, Vindicator, Vine, Virtuous, Vital, Vast

W With Us, Watches over Us, Worthy, Wise, Wisdom, Wealthy, Wonderful, Wonderful Counselor, Warrior, the Way, the Word, the Word of Life

X eXalted, eXcellent, eXceptional, eXample

Y Yahweh (Lord), Yahweh Sabaoth (Lord Almighty), Yeshua (God), Yearning for Us

Z Zealous, Zoologist, the God of Zion

Appendix E— More Names of God

Deeper Study

The Angel of Jehovah; Stone of Israel; Captain of the Host of the Lord; Rock of My Salvation; Light of the Morning; Tender Grass; Lifter of My Head; Jehovah—Mighty in Battle; King of Glory; My Strong Rock; Rock that Is Higher than I; Rain upon the Mown Grass; Showers upon the Earth; Head Stone of the Corner; Rose of Sharon; Lily of the Valley; Him Whom My Soul Loves; Chief among Ten Thousand; Wonderful; Counselor; Mighty God; Everlasting Father; Prince of Peace; My Strength and My Song; Nail Fastened in a Sure Place; Shadow from the Heat; Rock of Ages; Sure Foundation; King in His Beauty; Everlasting God; My Maker; God of the Whole Earth; Redeemer; My Physician; King over all the Earth; Prince of Princes; Son of David; Jesus; Son of Abraham; Emmanuel; Friend of Sinners; My Beloved; a Sower; Christ; Master; Bridegroom; Holy One of God; Our Brother; Son of the Most High; Carpenter; Good Master; Son of Man; Ransom; Son of the Highest; God the Savior; Dayspring from on High; Physician; Word; Light of Men; Lamb of God; Son of God; King of Israel; God's Only Begotten Son; Messiah; True Bread from Heaven; I Am; Door of the Sheep; Good Shepherd; One Shepherd; Resurrection; Way; Truth; Life; Vine; My Lord and My God; Lord Jesus; Lord of All; Judge of the Living and the Dead; God's Own Son; God Blessed Forever; Power of God; Wisdom of God; Our Passover; That Spiritual Rock; Lord from Heaven; Our Peace; Sweet Smelling Savor; Servant; the Image of the Invisible God; Creator of All Things; Head of the Body; Hope of Glory; Our Hope; God Manifest in the Flesh; Blessed and Only Potentate; the Righteous Judge; Great God; God Our Savior; Heir of All Things; Brightness of His Glory; God; the Captain of Our Salvation; Apostle; High Priest; Great High Priest; Priest Forever; Author of Eternal Salvation; Our Intercessor; He that Shall Come; Author and Finisher of Our Faith; My Helper; Jesus Christ the Same Yesterday, Today, and Forever; Living Stone; Chief Cornerstone; Precious Stone; Day Star; Word of Life; Advocate; Savior of the World; True God; Faithful Witness; Alpha and Omega; Almighty; First and Last; He that Lives; Morning Star; Amen; Lion of the Tribe of Judah; Holy and True; Lamb in the Midst of the Throne; King of Saints; Lord of Lords; King of Kings, Lord God Omnipotent

Deeper Study

Appendix F— Examples of Things to Pray

▲ SELF

▲ Thank You for making me the person that I am.

▲ Help me grow in my knowledge of You, God.

▲ Help me choose books, movies, and music to enjoy that honor You.

▲ Protect me from evil influences.

▲ Help me establish a regular prayer and devotion time.

⊛ PARENTS

⊛ Thank You for my parents and all that they do for me.

⊛ Keep their marriage strong, and protect it from things that would tear it apart.

⊛ Give them courage to say no to my requests if that is what is best for me.

⊛ Help them grow in their faith in Christ.

⊛ Give them wisdom in how they manage the family finances.

⊛ Give them patience with me and my brothers and sisters.

⊛ Bless the work they do for Your Kingdom.

⊛ Help them be good witnesses for You at work and in our town.

❖ FUTURE MATE

❖ Thank You that even now, You are preparing the man I will someday marry.

❖ I pray …that he will accept Christ as Savior and grow in his faith in Christ.

　　　…that he will stay pure for our marriage.

　　　…that he will choose a career that will use his God-given talents, one that honors You.

　　　…that he will stand firm against evil influences and against peer pressure.

❖ Help me become the young lady You want me to be, so I can be a loving, supportive wife to my future husband.

❑ FRIENDS/FRIENDSHIPS

❑ Thank You for the friends You have given me.

❑ Help me be a godly influence on my friends.

❑ Help me be a good, kind, and loving friend.

❑ Help me choose friends wisely, friends who will encourage me to live a life of faith.

❑ Protect me from friends who would try to influence me to disobey You.

• SIBLINGS

- Thank You for my brothers and sisters. Life would be lonely without them!
- Help me show Christlike love to them.
- Help them grow in their lives of faith.
- Help us respect each other's uniqueness and differences.
- Help us learn to cooperate with each other.
- Help us resolve arguments peacefully.

❑ TEACHERS

- Thank You for my teachers and their willingness to teach kids.
- Give them patience and love for all students.
- Give them wisdom to teach what is right and true according to the Bible.
- Help them treat students fairly.
- Give them wisdom when they must discipline students.
- Cause their day to go smoothly, so they can be at their best when they teach my class.

✪ UNSAVED FRIENDS

- Thank You for giving me the opportunity to share my faith with people who don't know You.
- Help them see how my faith in Jesus affects the way I live.
- Create a hunger for You inside them.
- Bring people into their lives who can tell them about Jesus.
- Protect their lives, so they can have the chance to accept Christ's gift of salvation.

◆ FAMILY ISSUES/PROBLEMS

- Thank You for the way You can use family problems to help my family grow in our trust in You.
- Bring Bible verses to the minds of my family members to help them remember how we should act toward each other.
- Help us solve problems peacefully.
- Help us encourage each other and be extra patient when our family is facing a tough time.
- Help us find ways to be kind to each other.
- Help our family seek what You want and put each other's interests above our own selfish wants.

SCHOOLWORK, HOMEWORK, STUDIES, AND TESTS

- Thank You for the way school and schoolwork is preparing me to become an adult someday.
- Help me discover through schoolwork the gifts, talents, and interests You have given me.
- Help me gain self-discipline in getting my homework done.
- Help me develop good study skills.
- Help me enjoy my time in school.
- Help me sleep well on the night before tests.

▼PRESSURES OF LIFE, STRESS

- ▼ Thank You for being with me, even when life gets stressful.
- ▼ When I worry, remind me of Bible verses that tell me You are with me always.
- ▼ Forgive me when I worry and fail to trust You with my problems.
- ▼ Help me put You first in my life, even when my life is stressful.

❖CHURCH

- ❖ Thank You for my church and church leaders. Thank You for their love and dedication to You.
- ❖ Protect the pastor and other leaders from Satan's attacks.
- ❖ Bring people to my church who need to know You and Your Son, Jesus, better.
- ❖ Use me to help my church grow.
- ❖ Help my Sunday-school teacher to teach the Bible clearly.
- ❖ Use me to encourage my pastor and other leaders of my church.
- ❖ Help the pastor in his sermons to teach the Bible clearly and accurately.
- ❖ Help the church leaders make wise decisions that honor You.

☆NATIONAL LEADERS

- ☆ Thank You for our country's leaders who are willing to be in tough positions to make this country strong.
- ☆ Give them energy and endurance to do their jobs.
- ☆ Give them courage to do what is right rather than what is popular.
- ☆ Help them react wisely when bad things happen in our country.
- ☆ Give them *lots* of wisdom when they make decisions.

✳ MISSIONARIES

✳ Thank You for those people who are so willing to leave home, friends, and this country, so they can tell people about Jesus.

✳ Protect them from harm.

✳ Provide for their needs of food, shelter, and friendship.

✳ Keep them from becoming discouraged.

✳ Show me how I can help a missionary.

✳ Help them understand the culture of the people, so they can tell about Jesus in a way the people will understand.

✿ SICKNESS AND CRISIS NEEDS

✿ Thank You that You are with this person.

✿ Thank You for this chance I have to show Your love and care for this person.

✿ Help this person learn to trust in You more during this hard time.

✿ If this person is a Christian, help others see how this person believes in You even when facing a hard time.

✿ Help others who are watching this person want to accept Jesus as their Savior.

✿ Bring people into this person's life who will encourage him or her.

✿ Show me how I can help this person during this difficult time.

✿ Use this situation to show how powerful You are, God.

Deeper Study

Appendix G—
God's Free Gift to You: The Gift of Salvation

Did you know that you can have a personal relationship with God like Millie does! The God that Millie Keith loves so much is the God of the whole universe. He is the One who created Heaven and Earth and everything in them, and He created you! He made you just the way you are, and He loves you so much that His love cannot be expressed fully in words.

Not only does God watch over you day and night, but He thinks about you all the time. God wants you to know Him personally and intimately. He longs for you to spend time with Him so that He can tell you how much He loves you. He wants to confide in you and tell you the secrets of His heart. And He wants you to share with Him the details of your life, because He cares about them. He wants to be your very, very best friend—closer to you than any human friend could ever be. In fact, God wants to be so close to you that He is willing to come and live inside you—right inside your heart. (That sounds impossible to us, but He can do that because He's God, and nothing is impossible for Him!)

God wants to give you a free gift—the gift of forgiveness of your sins and eternal life with Him. It is a gift that no one can earn or buy. Although it cost God a great price—the death of His beloved Son—for you it is really and truly free. All you have to do is accept the gift. You don't have to work hard or do anything to earn it.

If you want to have a personal relationship with God—a genuinely close relationship like you would have with a very intimate friend—you can have one right now, no matter how young or old you are. All you have to do is accept the gift of Jesus Christ's death on the Cross for your sins, believe in Him with all your heart, and believe God raised Him from the dead.

> If you confess with your mouth, "Jesus is Lord," and believe in your heart that God raised him from the dead, you will be saved. —ROMANS 10:9

Then you will discover something really amazing: Jesus is *alive*! Even though He died on the Cross in front of many, many witnesses, because He had no sin in Him He was raised back to life! Death had no right to hold on to Him! Jesus is *alive* today—He is a *living God*.

And if you invite Him to, He will send His Holy Spirit to live inside your heart. You will never be separated from Him again. We call this "becoming a Christian" and "being saved," because you are saved from the penalty of death and eternal separation from God.

You see, sin is what separates us from a relationship with God. A "sin" is what it is called when a person breaks one of God's laws or rules. God is perfect and holy—completely pure and without sin—and God cannot draw close to people with sin. You might not think of yourself as a sinner, but because of the sin of Adam and Eve, you (along with all human beings) were born with a sinful nature. You might not have committed *big* sins like murder, but at times you have probably committed *little* sins—like being mean, selfish, disobedient, impatient, untruthful, ungrateful, or unkind, or you may have done other things that are wrong in God's eyes. For it is God, not man, who determines what is right and what is wrong. Whether a person's sins are big or little doesn't matter because everything that falls short of God's standards is sin. Doing good deeds can never erase your sins (or get you into Heaven).

> All have sinned and fall short of the glory of God. —ROMANS 3:23
>
> It is by grace you have been saved, through faith—and this not from yourselves, it is the gift of God—not by works, so that no one can boast.
>
> —EPHESIANS 2:8–9

But, as we mentioned, God has free gifts for you—the gift of *forgiveness*, for all the sins you have ever committed, and the gift of *salvation*, which is deliverance from the power of sin. God is able to give you this incredible free gift because of His Son, Jesus Christ. Jesus died on the Cross and bore the punishment for your sin and for the sins of all mankind. You see, God is a God of justice, so all sin has to be punished. The penalty for sin is death—spiritual death here on Earth (which is not being in relationship with God) and physical death after life on Earth (which is eternal separation from God in a place called hell). But He doesn't want that! *God wants you to be spiritually alive right now and later spend eternity with Him in Heaven!*

When we give our hearts to Jesus and accept salvation, we begin a journey with God. On the journey, we learn more about what God's forgiveness really means to us personally. We begin the process of overcoming sin and temptation in our daily lives. We learn more about God's great love and plan for our lives, and we can live free from the worry of death and separation from God.

> God so loved the world that he gave his one and only Son, that whoever believes in him shall not perish but have eternal life.   —JOHN 3:16
>
> Christ died for sins once for all, the righteous for the unrighteous, to bring you to God. —1 PETER 3:18
>
> The wages of sin is death, but the gift of God is eternal life in Christ Jesus our Lord. —ROMANS 6:23
>
> God demonstrates his own love for us in this: While we were still sinners, Christ died for us. —ROMANS 5:8

Once you have made a heartfelt decision that you want to become a Christian and be saved, it is as simple as saying a prayer to God. You can say it in your own words, or you can pray the following simple prayer, either alone or with another Christian:

Dear Heavenly Father,

I know that I am a sinner and have often done things that are wrong. I am sorry for my sins and I ask You to forgive me for them. I accept the free gift of Jesus' death on the Cross in my place. I believe that Jesus died for my sins and was raised from the dead. I invite You—Father, Son, and Holy Spirit—to come live inside my heart and change me for the better. I give my life to You right now, and I ask that from this day forth, You would help me to follow You, to love You more and more, and to get to know You better. Amen.

If you prayed to accept Jesus, now you can look forward to a wonderful relationship with the Living God! Your sins have been washed away, and you have been *born again*. (The first time you were born physically; this time you were born spiritually.) Write down today's date, for it is your spiritual birthday and you will want to remember it!

Here are some simple steps to do once you have accepted Christ into your heart:

Tell someone else (preferably another Christian) about the commitment you just made to the Lord. If that someone else is not your parent, then you should also tell your mother or father (or your guardian). If he or she is not a Christian, then you might want to show this section to them and have them read it too. It will help them to understand the commitment you have made and why you have made it.

Talk to God in prayer. You can speak to Him openly and honestly, at any time of the day or night, as often as you want to. Pray for yourself as well as for other people. Tell God what is on your heart and mind. Ask Him for wisdom and guidance when you need it. He loves you and is interested in your needs, your desires, and the details of your life. Learn to share your life with Him. Be quick to ask for God's forgiveness if and when you sin. And take time regularly to thank Him for His many blessings.

Get your own copy of the Holy Bible, the Word of God, in a translation that you can understand. Read from it every day. (A good place to start is the New Testament book of John.) Study the Scriptures and memorize your favorite verses. Expect God to speak to you through His Word.

Find a church that teaches the Bible and attend it regularly. Get involved in a home Bible study group.

Get water baptized. Talk to your pastor and parents about this.

Seek out other Christians in your school or at work or in other places, and develop new friendships.

Tell others about your love for the Lord.

Guard your heart and do not let other people or other things steal your faith in and love for God.

Enjoy your relationship with Jesus!

Collect all of our Millie products!

A Life of Faith: Millie Keith Series

Collect our other *A Life of Faith* Products!

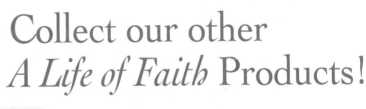

A Life of Faith: Elsie Dinsmore

Beloved Literary Characters

Come to Life!

$\mathcal{Y}$our favorite heroines, Elsie Dinsmore and Millie Keith, are now available as lovely designer dolls from Mission City Press.

$\mathcal{M}$ade of soft-molded vinyl, these beautiful, fully-jointed 18¾" dolls come dressed in historically-accurate clothing and accessories. They wonderfully reflect the Biblical virtues that readers have come to know and love about Elsie and Millie.

For more information, visit www.alifeoffaith.com or check with your local Christian retailer.

A Life of Faith
Products from Mission City Press

"It's Like Having a Best Friend From Another Time"

Check Out

www.alifeoffaith.com

- Get news about Millie and her cousin Elsie
- Find out more about the 19th century world they live in
- Learn to live a life of faith like they do
- Learn how they overcome the difficulties we all face in life
- Find out about Millie and Elsie products
- Join our girls' club

A Life of Faith Books

"It's Like Having a Best Friend From Another Time"